Beyond Eden

The Mysteries of His New Name

Amy Thomas Davis

Foreword Paul Keith Davis

BookLocker
Trenton, Georgia

Print ISBN: 978-1-959624-56-1
Ebook ISBN: 979-8-88532-123-5

Published by BookLocker.com, Inc., Trenton, Georgia.

BookLocker.com, Inc.
2025

First Edition

Copyright page to give cover design credit to Halle Hendrix, Maggie Jones, and Lisa Maria Green

Library of Congress Cataloging in Publication Data
Davis, Amy Thomas
Beyond Eden: The Mysteries of His New Name by
Amy Thomas Davis
Library of Congress Control Number: 2025916755

Beyond Eden is a tribute to every child of every generation who has been violated, abused, or trafficked. God will bring His retributive justice.

To the brave survivors, I pray for God to encounter you and heal you with His unfailing love. This book is dedicated to you.

FOREWORD
By Paul Keith Davis

A great novelist once wrote, "It was the best of times, it was the worst of times." Long before Charles Dickens immortalized those words in his classic novel, the Bible foretold those very conditions when describing the final generation before the return of Jesus Christ. It will be a time of unparalleled darkness and brilliant light.

For millennia, the influences of spiritual darkness have operated in subterfuge, hidden away in the unspoken corners of culture. Now those dark and sinister entities can no longer hide. They are being brought into the Light, unmasked and identified. That is the noble mandate of this book! Not only are realms of darkness exposed, they are overruled by the great truth given to us in God's word through the power of the Holy Spirit reserved for the consummation of this age.

Virtually every segment of our society is asking the same question as they navigate 21st-century culture, including political alignments, geological tragedies, and cultural chaos. What does this mean? Interestingly, 2000 years ago, the same question was asked when God's Spirit was sent to the earth following thc dcath, burial, and resurrection of Jesus Christ.

This is recorded in Acts 2. The people of that generation experienced something unprecedented and unfamiliar. Men and women were filled with a supernatural Presence that gave them great joy, and they were speaking in foreign languages they had no way of knowing by natural means. Observers then asked the right questions, "What does this mean? What shall we do?

Those are valid questions that must also be asked today, involving the many provocative issues that we uniquely face. Fortunately, Amy has written a book that will provide answers to both of those strategic questions. She goes into great detail to explain the meaning of current events and explicitly outlines how we should respond biblically and thereby successfully.

Being married to Amy, I've watched firsthand as she's carried this book in her creative womb, being nurtured, birthed, and championed with a profound message that will distinctly influence a generation. I am more qualified than any to validate the prophetic mantle on her life and the consistent accuracy by which the Lord has spoken to her. That is a very important foundation as we broach the spiritually sensitive subjects of “The Last Days."

According to some demographics, almost 50% of Americans believe we are living in what the Bible describes as "the end times." Furthermore, 67% of evangelical Christians confirm this reality. Fortunately, the Bible has devoted considerable portions to the subject. The Lord Himself predicted a time of wars, earthquakes, plagues, famines, and other dramatic events to highlight the final generation, along with the pathway to victory during these turbulent times. Biblical prophets also foretold a time of heightened spiritual conflict where previous boundaries and limitations are lifted.

It is almost as if a new vocabulary has been created to articulate ancient spiritual conflicts that were very prevalent during the antediluvian era but hidden for many centuries. Now the curtain has been lifted and these ancient spiritual realities are made a part of current conversation. The times dictate greater maturity and a working knowledge of spiritual principles that have only previously been addressed in fringe elements of modern spirituality. This was affirmed by the words of the Lord Jesus when He said, "as it was in the days of Noah so shall it be at the coming of the Son of Man."

The years leading up to Noah's flood witnessed unparalleled spiritual wickedness involving entities from the unseen realm cohabitating with humanity. This is explicitly detailed in both the Old and New Testament narratives. The corruption that existed during that timeline was so complete that a global flood was necessary to purge the earth in order for a new beginning to be established. Those are the spiritual criteria given to us to help highlight the spiritual climate of this age.

Even so, the many biblical references talking about this generation emphasize a profound grace coming from God that can be experienced personally and corporately. A time of divine visitation and prophetic fulfillment that can only be matched by the first-century church. That is the hope of our calling and the eternal purpose to be achieved in this final generation.

God's people are promised a literal utopia even greater than the original Garden of Eden, once occupied by Adam and Eve. We see it described in the book of Revelation. Even so, getting to this place in human history will require one final spiritual conflict with realms of darkness that must be overcome. The Bible describes it as the greatest spiritual war in 6000 years of human history. We are seeing the initial evidence of that animosity even now.

God is equipping a community of people with great spiritual insight and biblical understanding in order to "overcome" the rulers and authorities that are trying to prevent the reality of a restored Eden. Our Messiah, the last Adam, will return to this earth in one final display of glory to fulfill all biblical prophecy. Understanding this confrontation is the heart of Amy's book. In the original Eden, there was a unique working relationship between God and His people to rule and subdue the earth. This exchange continued following the fall of man, involving men and women who represented God's Kingdom on the earth in an ongoing conflict with realms of darkness.

God has chosen the agency of man to accomplish His eternal purpose. Likewise, the enemy of all that is good also uses mankind to advance his agenda in his ruthless attempt to circumvent God's plan. This provides the root issue that will reach its pinnacle in this final generation.

This and much more is included in Beyond Eden. Amy has captured glimpses of God's heart and understanding to help posture a foreknown generation for great spiritual advancement—a people who will be rescued from the domain of darkness and transferred into the Kingdom of Light.

INTRODUCTION

The mysteries of Eden will be discovered by the overcoming end-time generation, who will understand His glory Light. They desire not the light of stages or platforms, for they are emerging in the Light of the Lamb, in tune with the value of restored Eden and the Light of God, which empowers the garden.

The prophet Daniel prophesied that a generation would come in the final days who would understand the brightness of His appearing and would eternally shine like the radiant expanse of heaven, leading many to righteousness. Daniel was instructed to seal his prophecy until the end of time for a specific generation that would access the mind of God's Spirit and increase in the knowledge of God and the true nature of His name. (Daniel 12:3-4) The fullness of time has come for the demonstration of glory that Daniel prophesied. Hidden truths that have been set apart are now being revealed to a chosen remnant; truth that spans beyond this realm and introduces mysteries of the Kingdom age and beyond. These mysteries are preparing the bride for His return and the fulfillment of our eternal purpose in Him.

According to Revelation 1:8, 21:6, and 22:13, the Lord is the Alpha and thc Omcga, thc bcginning and thc cnd, who was, and is, and is to come. He will reveal His power in a distinct way at the end of the age, as Omega, which will differ from His initial manifestation in the beginning as Alpha. The champions of the last days are the Omega generation, foreknown and predestined to participate in the Lord's Omega plans when they fully embrace their identity in Christ as He reveals Himself as Omega.

The Omega people hold fast to His name and understand His nature in the last days and express His glory Light amidst a dark and wicked era. Drawing from His attributes, they will fulfill over 2,000 end-of-the-age Bible prophecies dealing with Omega, the future age, and beyond. They are called for this purpose to usher in the end-time harvest and introduce
the coming age, and to transition the bride into the next phase of our eternal purpose in God.

Revelation 20 explains the future age and the events that precede it. This epoch is a one-thousand-year reign of Christ, during which priests of God will reign with Him for a thousand years in the restored Eden. The serpent will not be in the garden but will be sealed into an abyss, unable to deceive the people. The dragon, the serpent of old, who is the devil and Satan, is bound for one thousand years. During this age, the nations will resort to Christ the Lord, who stands as a signal flag and a resting place for the people. The sevenfold nature of God is the standard in the garden, and His Spirit will rest upon the people. The Spirit of wisdom and understanding, the Spirit of Counsel and Strength, the Spirit of Knowledge, and the Fear of the Lord. And the people will walk in the Light of God (Isaiah 11).

Although the millennial kingdom takes place in a different era, Hebrews 6:5 clearly indicates that some from this generation will taste God's Word and experience His power in the restored garden of Eden, which is the future age. This is a privilege of the overcomers who are partakers of the Bread of Life by the

Spirit of God. As forerunners, they draw from the future age and prophecy the new day for the reaping of the harvest and preparation of the bride for His appearing. They encompass Restored Eden and walk with God in glorious realms, discovering the power of his energy.

The life of Omega that now is and the life in the coming epoch are the profit of godly living (1 Timothy 4:8). Vibrant life and light consume the restored garden and are accessible to those who walk with God. It is this energy that fuels the Omega generation as they taste the good Word of God and the powers of the age to come.

Eden is a place of order and holy conduct, where the sons of God and all creation live in concord and dwell amongst the God of nations. The Omega generation who lives on the earth in the final age has been permitted access to this realm for equipping and to receive the nourishment from the light of God to withstand the darkest days of humanity.

We are living in Omega time; it is imperative that we understand the environment of the last days and the intensity of the spiritual conflict to overcome the spirit of the age and receive our inheritance in Christ. As the Omega generation, we will partake of His Word and experience His power through the indwelling of His presence to make known His manifold wisdom to the principalities and powers that manifest in the dark world. This responsibility is an integral part of our eternal purpose in Christ and is accomplished through divine cooperation and in fellowship with God.

There has been a gradual increase of knowledge throughout the ages, through the heroes of the faith who await the empowerment of our generation, so that we may all be made perfect. We no longer identify with the hopelessness of the religion of previous eras; it is the fullness of time for the Omega generation to emerge in the true knowledge of God and opportunely draw from the fruit of the land.

In this book, Beyond Eden: The Mysteries of His New Name, we will delve into complex questions and expose previously hidden truths that God has reserved for this generation to equip us to overcome the spirit of the age and fulfill our eternal purpose in Him. We can no longer remain in ignorance regarding the culture of this age and the darkness that covers the Earth. The Spirit of the Lord calls the sons of God to overcome the spirit of the age by the Spirit of Truth. Those who align with the spiritual truth of this book will embark on a journey into Restored Eden and beyond, to experience the Light of the Lord, prayerfully encountering Him to be equipped to fulfill the divine destiny of the bride.

CHAPTER 1

I am the flame above the beauty in the fields; I shine in the waters; I burn in the sun, the moon, and the stars. And with the airy wind, I quicken all things vitally by an unseen, all-sustaining life.

~Hildegard von Bingen

A DWELLING PLACE

The Light of Life draws us into our eternal purpose, and through His life force, we experience spiritual growth, enabling us to become pure light and shine brilliantly in His image. He is the Father of lights, with whom there is no variation or shifting shadow. Holding fast to His name, we enter His essence and become the bursting forth of the Light of life to overcome death and emerge into our destiny to dwell as one in Him. Life in His image is everlasting, and we move from glory to glory, unlocking the mystery of His new name.

The Spirit of God has made us, and the breath of the Almighty has given life. And we all, with unveiled face, beholding the glory of the Lord, are being transformed into the same image from one degree of glory to another. Every phase of our existence prepares us for the next level of glory as we embody His divine nature and explore the wonders of His Spirit. By His Spirit, our spirit moves through each phase of our eternal purpose, continuously emerging in the Light of the Lamb to ultimately dwell together with Him in perfect union forever as the Wife of the Lamb, adorned by the brilliance of His splendor.

The Lord is preparing a dwelling place for union with His bride. All of creation will be transformed, and the Garden of Eden will be restored to greater glory, and we will dwell in union with Him for one thousand years—this is the Kingdom Age. Every age leading up to the Kingdom age is a progression toward our eternal purpose, drawing us to a deeper level of union. Our destiny has not been fulfilled by our time on earth, nor with the completion of the Kingdom Age; there is a union beyond Eden.

Understanding Eden and what lies beyond is essential for our development. Eden is both a reward for those who overcome in this life and also an introduction to God's ultimate intentions for His bride. Though the Garden of Eden is in the future age and will be restored, it must also be accessed in the spirit now for the preparation of the Bride of Christ. Surveying the age to come and captivating the nature of this realm, we are further empowered for the advancement of the Kingdom.

THE LIGHT OF THE FUTURE AGE

Eden is a perfect state of existence, where the Light of God shines from the essence of all creation, radiating from the land. The Spirit of Life is intricately woven into every aspect. The garden is a perfect balance of strength and elegance, an intelligent cooperation of all things good, derived from the knowledge of God. We are all emerging into the true knowledge of our eternal purpose in Christ, which is for union. He is intimately acquainted with the ways of creation and has purposefully designed this dwelling place for His beloved to engage intimately with Him.

The Garden is an array of effervescent light. Everything in Restored Eden is an energy source created to glorify the Creator, which glows harmoniously in multi-color on a wavelength superior to Earth. Each hue a representation of the divine splendor of the throne of God. I was permitted to visit the future age and eat of the fruit of this land, tasting "the good word of God and the powers of the age to come." This particular fruit was not fruit at all, as we would imagine it to be, but an element of light producing a virtue of His Spirit.

Spiritual living beings are in various forms in the garden, each one shining by the light of His glory. Two women were there, Eve and another young lady who led me to the land. The young lady is beautiful in appearance and radiates the Spirit of God. She was steady and balanced by the light and sound of this place, moving in perfect rhythm with nature and the seasons of Eden.

Eden is plentiful yet not crowded and rests atop a high mountain with a steep incline, presumably the holy mountain of God. A mountain beyond the reach of the heavenly skies, but with a vastness of its own. Where the garden is illuminated with the fire glory of God, and grace drips like dew on every member. I was powerfully impacted by the fruit of the land and the expression of the virtues of God in each element. I understood what Ezekiel saw and recorded (Ezekiel 28:14). He replays the conflict in the original garden of Eden and expresses the beauty of this place, describing Eden as the garden on the holy mountain of God with stones of fire covering the land. I, too, saw flaming, colorful embers along the ground and growing within the garden as foliage and bloom.

The two ladies introduced me to Eden. The young lady of Eden was the main guide. She moved us through the garden barefoot and confident, describing the true nature and life source of the restored Garden. She held the greatest knowledge of Eden, even greater than Eve's knowledge. The young lady of Eden directed me to eat from the land, perceiving that I needed it. God filled every element of the garden, but I was only permitted to eat a particular kind of fruit, which was in season, a large grape the size of a tangerine, radiant with the light of God. The taste was perfect. Courage filled me—courage that would carry me through the next season of my life.

Eve is a woman of many firsts, including the first woman to experience the glory of God in the original Garden of Eden. She did not understand the future garden as entirely as the young lady. It appeared she did not have the same knowledge or access. I realized Eve knew the original garden. The young lady of Eden knows the future garden.

SEASONS OF EDEN

Restored Eden is abundant in energy and balanced by order. Everything is alive with wonder and purpose and is given an opportunity to manifest the presence of God. The energy source from within creation pulsates eternally like a heartbeat. The pulse intensifies in season, bringing the member into full shine. The stars shine in season as the main event, followed by the produce of the land and the stones of the earth. The seasons of Eden are for the radiant display of His beauty.

The Life source for the garden is the Light of God. All of God's creation is compelled to shine for Him. The stars in the sky are like a garden in the heavens that expresses its light until the duration of that season is complete. Then, the gardens, including the fruits, plants, and flowers, become as the firmament. The rhythm of Eden is cyclical. Creation takes turns in the expression of His glory. The warm glow from the fruit of the garden lingers until their season is complete. These seasons last longer than the season of the stars.

ABIDE

In this realm, the beloved is drawn to abide in harmony with each other and in union with God. It is abounding in lovingkindness, devoted in honor and love, preferring one to another without arrogance. Eden is the embodiment of servitude, grace, and order, which are pleasing to God. I recognized the young lady of Eden carries these same attributes. I presume it is the result of dwelling in His presence, which illuminates all things and draws every element of the Kingdom into one accord.

Hildegard von Bingen, a German poet and mystic visionary from the Middle Ages, had remarkable revelations about God's Garden through multiple visions and encounters. She expressed her insights about the divine works of God through her poetry and other literary works, including those on holistic medicine, botanical studies, and natural science. She understood that all of creation works together for His glory, stating, "God has arranged everything in the universe in consideration of everything else." This phenomenon brings order to the

Kingdom of God. Christ holds it all together; it was the Father's good pleasure for all the fullness to dwell in Him. The purpose of creation is to serve and prefer in love as reverence to God, which is an acceptable service.

The young lady of Eden was knowledgeable about the seasons and where to draw from the assemblage of life for each circumstance. With unparalleled revelation, she grasps the true nature of the restored garden, which she utilized to guide me to the necessary fruit. Good fruit for the occasion is likened to a fitly spoken word in due season, carried back into the realm of time and applied appropriately.

She is a forerunner and representation of the end of this age community who will travel to and fro to increase in the knowledge of God, so to shine before men like the brightness of the expanse of heaven, and lead many to righteousness like the stars forever and ever. Compelled to shine in due season, they will access the future age and learn the order and function of the garden to then model those attributes on the earth.

THE EXERTION OF ENERGY

It is essential to learn the function of the coming age, and from that knowledge, we are further equipped to operate in our God given authority on the earth. The Garden of Eden, in the coming age, operates from the life energy of God, which is a constant source that ignites all creation. The energy of God compels creation to reveal His glory. The testimonies of the miracles of glory will be evidence of the outworking of His energy, which is known and accessible in the garden, and empowers the Sons of Light. Walking with God in glorious realms, we are transformed by His virtues. As we encompass the energy of God in Eden, we discover Life with every turn.

Spiritual energy is a generative force that exerts power in the individual, both in life and in death, depending on the nature of the source. Spiritual life energy is the power of God, which energized Christ with resurrection power. Ephesians 1:20 reveals the energy of the Spirit of Might that raised Jesus from the dead.

"And what is the surpassing greatness of His power toward us who believe? These are by the working of the strength of His might which He brought about (energized) in Christ when He raised Him from the dead and seated Him at His right hand in the heavenly places."

Previous eras have hidden from the energy of God and feared the testing of His power. The Omega generation engages with God and His Spirit of Might to the bursting forth of light. The word *energy* in the New Testament is the Greek word *energeo* (from energeia), meaning *engaged in*, which is appropriately translated *energize*, working in a situation that brings it from one stage to the next, like an electrical current energizing a wire, bringing it to a shining light bulb.

The word energize is used interchangeably in many verses in the New Testament with words that represent an *effective work*, *to exert*, or *to bring about*. The spiritual realm consists of energies, both good and evil. God's Spirit is bringing about abundant blessings in harmony with His virtues and attributes, including spiritual life. Life energy is an eternal energy that motivates the sons of God into their eternal purposes. With this understanding, let's pay close attention to Ephesians 3:20,

"Now to Him who is able to do far more abundantly beyond all that we ask or think, according to the power that works (energizes) within us."

The same life energy dwells within the garden and empowers the sons of light to illuminate the surrounding darkness of the world, a brilliance that darkness cannot comprehend. Satan is working to thwart the eternal purposes and light of God through fallen entities that empower the unrighteous through dark world energies. Ephesians 2:1-3 expresses the enemy's involvement with the unrighteous to carry out the desires of the flesh.

"And you He made alive, who were dead in trespasses and sins, in which you once walked according to the course of this world, according to the prince of the power of the air, the spirit who is now working in (energizes) the sons of disobedience, among whom also we all once conducted ourselves in the lusts of our flesh, fulfilling the desires of the flesh and of the mind, and were by nature children of wrath, just as the others."

The enemy is the prince of the *exousia* power of the air. This is not the same *dunamis* power that God is working with in us. *Exousia* means authority or jurisdiction. This verse in Ephesians 2 does not signify a power over the air but a ruler dwelling in a region of the air, and more technically indicates a superhuman ruler. Specifically, a dark and evil superhuman power that has been allowed to encompass and move above the world but is overruled by the true *dunamis* that is in God.

God has energized His power in His sons, the same power that is in the life of the garden. The enemy has been given authority as the prince of the power of the air for an allotted time. Ultimately, the devil loses his power. Until then, the *dunamis* of God energizes the righteous sons of God to be the restraining force that pushes back the darkness. The Omega generation is that restraining force, enduring the darkest years of humanity.

DUNAMIS

It is imperative to understand the power of His might that operates through us to overcome the spirit of this age that has been given authority in the earth for a time. Satan has *exousia* (authority); he does not have *dunamis* (power). For many eras, the body of Christ has been operating in limited authority equal to or even less than the power of the enemy. In ignorance, the church assumed its power came from religious traditions or popularity. Though the church (as a whole) has missed it, several forerunners have operated in the Spirit of Might. They were a foreshadowing of what was to come when God pours out His Spirit in the end through the Omega generation, who have no concern for human self-will or traditions of man. We will operate in the *dunamis* of God, and He will be glorified in praise for the surpassing greatness of His power, which is of Him and not from ourselves.

Francis Metcalfe, a mystic known for her prophetic experiences and visions, was the founding member of Golden Candlestick, a covenant fellowship dedicated to worshiping the Lord and interceding for His bride. Francis Metcalfe was translated to heavenly realms and energized with the power of God for prayer, praise, and prophecy. She expressed her union experiences with God in her writings that she penned for this generation to glean from, as a forerunner of the Omega People. She emphasizes praise as a standard of living and for receiving and operating in the *dunamis* of God. In her booklet titled "Living the Life of Praise," she explains how this truth must be rediscovered with each generation for the release of His power.

"Some of the greatest discoveries the sons of God are making are in the realm of God's nuclear power — the *dunamis* of the Spirit. This omnipotent power — of which the nuclear energy in the physical universe is a fitting symbol — is released and channeled into the earth by faith and PRAISE. When God is actively, fervently, and continuously praised, this *dunamis* power is readily manifested. For praise provides a habitation, an atmosphere, in which God can move and act.

In both the Old and New Testaments there is much instruction about praising the Lord. But each generation seems to have to rediscover this truth. In the days of Israel's greatness, King David knew the secret of this power. Not only did he practice praise himself, but he taught all Israel how to praise God. And he set apart several thousand chosen ones to be trained to minister continually unto the Lord in praise.

This power of praise was likewise known and manifested in the Christian Church, both in early and later days. It was prayer and praise that prepared the disciples for the descent of the Holy

Spirit on the Day of Pentecost and drew Him to their hearts. And in the succeeding ages, praise has again and again released this power on earth."

THE SEED

The energy of God is in all of creation and is visible in the restored garden; however, only the Sons of God carry the special seed of God. The seed of God is like a pulsating heartbeat within the Sons of Light. It is energized by His eternal power to reveal the true knowledge of His divine nature. As the seed is activated, the blessing pours out like a river of gold liquid bursting from the innermost being.

We are emerging in the eternal purpose of God, which is in the seed of God. The eternal purpose of God is not an event that takes place one day in the future when our time on earth is over. Eternity is the overarching dimension of God from which the children of God exist. God is eternal. Isaiah 43:3 says, "Even from eternity I am He." Each stage of our existence progresses from eternity to eternity like an unending circle. We grow like the sprouting of a seed into our ultimate call, which is for absolute oneness.

The eternal realm enables us to fulfill our upward calling on the earth while in the mortal body until we put on the imperishable. The realm of time is not a restriction or a hindrance; it is for order. All of creation co-operates in divine order so that His purpose is established in the earth. In these moments, eternity and time overlap. This is the fringes of His glory, even to taste the powers of the age to come, which enable us to complete our work on the earth, until we move into the next dimension of our eternal existence. Ultimately, our purpose in Him is to dwell as one. This is no longer to cooperate, but to operate in absolute perfection with one another and in union with God.

ETERNAL RHYTHM

The rhythmic frequencies of heaven continually radiate from creation because of the power of life within. The rhythm of His Spirit causes every element in the garden to move in concord with everything else He has created.

All creation within the Kingdom of God is a complex layering of eternal rhythms, like a wheel within a wheel, representing realms of eternity with living spirit within. The rhythmic frequency of God is a visible radiance surrounding every creation, filled and corralled by His goodness.

The voice of the Almighty surges through the river in Eden. The water of the river of God is a well springing up to eternal life. It is established in the rhythm of God and brings healing and spirit life energy to all who enter. The river of life energizes the sons of God with immortality, just as the Spirit of God energized the Christ for resurrection and to be seated at His right hand.

The Bride of Christ is awakening to our purpose through divine rhythm. This rhythm is an everlasting progression which calls to our spirit like deep unto deep, moving us into perfect connection with Him. This eternal union began in Him, and we who have His seed are born of Him. We move through many stages of existence. These stages do not end when this world ends, and did not begin when this world began. We came forth from the dwelling of eternal light, born into the likeness of God to be sons of light and sons of the day. Job 38 says, "Where is the way to the dwelling of light and darkness, where is its place. Do you know because you were born then?" Our Spirit, which is eternal, is birthed of the everlasting Light.

Though we are in a temporary mortal body, we will inherit the imperishable. (1 Peter) The fire of God will eternally burn in our midst, lighting the atmosphere as He displays His glory through us in Eden for one thousand years. Ultimately, He reveals the new heaven and new earth, and we will come out of heaven as the Holy City with the Light of the Lamb in our midst, forever. As we overcome, we emerge into this purpose, God will render to every man accordingly, crowns, treasures, and everlasting life.

CHAPTER 2

Our hearts yearn for a return to the Garden. We sing a wailing song of remembrance. Selah. If we pause, we might hear the Garden crying for us.

~John L. Moore

IMMORTALITY

The Spirit of Life runs through Eden, like blood through the veins of man. Every morsel an aspect of the Life which is in God. The Spirit of Life is boundless and transcends the fleeting nature of time and the vastness of space, represented in the openness of Eden's landscape, which appears to have unending rolling hills and fields of glowing flowers. The young lady of Eden is of the immortal ones who carry a revelation of the life in Eden, which is the Light of God. When in Eden, they flow in the rhythm of life, which is available through the river of life. They obtain knowledge from the Tree of Life, which is life in Christ and the true knowledge of God.

There is a select body of believers on Earth destined for eternal life and immortality through their walk with God. Like Christ, their flesh will not suffer decay, and when He appears, they will be caught up into Him for union. They will not taste death at all. They are a continuous display of His splendor, a mature people who will journey in the true light which enlightens every man.

As vessels of Light, regarded and formed from the very hands of God, each is energized by God after the counsel of His will to make known the riches of His glory. He forms them according to the spirit will of each person by His foreknowledge, and they obtain an inheritance, having been predestined according to His purpose and in His divine sovereignty, even to put on immortality and know deathlessness in Him.

Like Enoch, they desire to know immortality, believing they will not die. They will not die a first death nor a second death. Revelation 20 describes those who have died already and will be resurrected at the end of the age to rule and reign as priests of God and Christ in the millennial kingdom. They are blessed to experience the first resurrection and will not experience a second death. However, there is a community that will not taste death at all. They have a revelation to walk with God forever throughout this age, the marriage union, and into the coming epoch.

I ENOCH

It is recorded in the historical writings in I Enoch that Enoch was given a tour of the garden and inquired of the archangel Michael to learn about the Tree of Life, discerning the power of life in the fruit, which brings healing Light to all nations.

Undoubtedly, Enoch had a revelation that he would live and not die, motivating him to learn everything about life, especially about the Tree of Life. The historical writings of Enoch, according to I Enoch, describe his journey and the questions he had about the nature of the garden and the essence of life.

"And there was a tree such as which I have never smelt, and none of them, or any others, were like it. It smells more fragrant than any fragrance, and its leaves, and its flowers, and its wood never wither. Its fruit is good, and its fruit is like bunches of dates on a palm. And then I said: "Behold, this beautiful tree! Beautiful to look at, and pleasant are its leaves, and its fruit very delightful in appearance."

And then Michael, one of the Holy and honored Angels, who was with me, and was in charge of the trees, answered me and said to me: "Enoch, why do you ask me about the fragrance of this tree, and why do you inquire to learn?"

Then I, Enoch, answered him, saying: "I wish to learn about everything, but especially about this tree."

Enoch's quest to understand the garden and the tree is driven by his desire to fulfill his eternal purpose— to encompass the spirit of Life and dwell in union with God. Enoch's curiosity was not to please his flesh as was Eve's curiosity. Enoch desired to draw from the Life of the Garden and gain knowledge of God and His creation.

The archangel Michael responded to Enoch's desire for true knowledge by sharing a prophetic promise, which is likened to the many verses in the holy scriptures about the coming age and the life of future Eden, whose fruit is available to us. This promise depicts the last day generation, who, like Enoch, will captivate the nature of the garden and wear immortality like a fragrance that seeps deeply into their being, strengthening them to live and not die. They eagerly await, groaning not to divest the body but to renew it through glorification that mortality may be swallowed up by life, which is part of the eternal reward of those who desire the indwelling of the living God.

"From its fruit, life will be given to the chosen; towards the north it will be planted, in a Holy place, by the house of the Lord, the Eternal King. Then they will rejoice with joy and be glad in the Holy place. They will each draw the fragrance of it into their bones, and they will live a long life on earth, as your fathers lived. And in their days sorrow and pain, and toil and punishment, will not touch them. Then I blessed the Lord of Glory, the Eternal King, because he has prepared such things for righteous men, and has created such things, and said that they are to be given to them."

RETURN TO THE GARDEN

Our eternal purpose unfolds with each display of glory. The Garden of Eden in the beginning was an opportunity for perfect union and authority. Restored Eden is everything the first garden was and more. Eden is a sacred space. The place on earth God chose to meet with man. Like Zion, the Holy City, it is the dwelling place of God on earth. This excerpt from Paul Keith's writings beautifully encapsulates the nature of Eden and its participation in our eternal purpose.

"According to the Hebrew University, scholars are not precisely clear on the exact meaning of "Eden." Clearly, however, the root word translated Eden is used throughout the Scriptures and is consistently related to "pleasure" or "delight." Therefore, it is no surprise to discover that the Hebrew word to relate heaven or paradise on earth is "garden of Eden." The delightful and pleasurable place in which God dwells.

The story of Adam and Eve encompasses the authoritative position they were given that was lost through deception and sin. Woven within the very fabric of our souls to this very day is the yearning to return to that place of innocence and fellowship with God. It was the place where heaven touched earth, and Adam was charged with the responsibility of governing the earth on behalf of God's Kingdom.

Here, Adam exercised the full authority of sonship and enjoyed unencumbered fellowship with the Father in his stewardship of creation. We now have the amazing hope that Jesus said, "In My Father's house are many dwelling places." The Lord has now offered this tremendous privilege to His sons and daughters to rule and reign with Him in the age to come. This is the true concept of spiritual adoption — to be placed in our position of leadership in God's counsel and oversight of creation.

Embedded in ancient Mesopotamian culture is the idea of humans having fellowship with God on a sacred mountain or in the garden of Elohim. Many scholars believe that the original Garden of Eden geographically included Mount Hermon. It is noteworthy to point out that the prophet Ezekiel not only refers to Eden as the "garden of God" (Ezekiel 28:13-14) but also "the holy mountain of God".

This kind of language was common in ancient culture and is affirmed in Scripture as the chosen dwelling place of the Living God. So, while it is believed by most that the Garden of Eden was a literal location on the earth that was lush and beautiful, it was more importantly the meeting place with Elohim. The location of God's desire and His willingness to meet face-to-face with mankind in realms of glory (paradise)!

In the Lord's message to the Ephesian church recorded by John in his Patmos vision, the reward given to those who overcome is the privilege of eating from the Tree of Life, which is in the Paradise of God. This is a clear reference to what had once been lost but now restored. It is the promise of God for a generation of people to experience the delightfulness and pleasure of paradise for those who overcome.

Therefore, we can conclude that Eden is more than just a lush garden with beautiful trees and streams. More completely, it is the place of God's fellowship and the seat of His authority to govern the earth. Those who overcome not only eat from the Tree of Life, which is in the paradise of God, but they are also seated with Christ on His throne as He overcame to sit with the Father. It is for this reason that we are referred to as the sons of God and are adopted and placed into our authority as heirs of God by becoming partakers of the divine nature. From this place we are promised to share in His authority to rule the nations with a rod of iron."— Paul Keith Davis

CHAPTER 3

Glorious things of thee are spoken, Zion, city of our God!

John Newton

THE LIVING STONE

The young lady of Eden has significance beyond the restored garden. She is of the Omega Generation who lives through the transition of the ages; she is also a daughter of Zion. The Zion company is a remnant of the chosen people of God emerging in the light of true knowledge. The seed of God abides in Zion— It is the imperishable and prosperous seed birthed through the living and enduring Word of God by the spotless blood of Jesus Christ.

Zion is privileged to learn the mysteries that for ages past were hidden in God. The destiny of this royal priesthood is to commune with God at a depth other people have not experienced, to forerun the eternal union. The Lord Jesus ministered to a great multitude, yet only a few walked with Him intimately. So will it be for the remnant of God's people.

"If it is marvelous in the eyes of the remnant of this people in these days, will it also be marvelous in My eyes?" Says the Lord of Hosts. (Zechariah 8:6)

Zion will break forth like the dawn to raise up the foundation of the generations. They are as living stones built as sacrifices acceptable to God. Jesus is the Cornerstone, and He is the

Capstone that has been laid in Zion. He is the first and the last, the beginning and the end. The hands of Zerubbabel have laid the foundation, and His hands shall complete it. He will bring forth the top stone, which is the capstone, to complete the work of His holy mountain.

The living stones are the Zion people throughout the ages who are being formed into Him and are a living sacrifice acceptable to God. God is revealing Himself through the Capstone generation, which is the Omega generation at the end of the age; He will finish what He has started. For the Lord has chosen Zion; he has desired it for his dwelling place. The appointed time has come to take pleasure in her stones, which are the living stones, the righteous generation. The Lord will make them a blessing, fearless and strong, and He will arise and have mercy on Zion and glorify her.

MOUNT ZION

On the day that the Lord gave the Mosaic Covenant to His people, Israel, He warned that those who approached the mountain would die. Only Moses could come to the mountain to accept His law. Mount Sinai, a mountain so terrifying that Moses said, "I am exceedingly afraid and trembling." We are no longer a people separated from God's presence, as the Israelites who were at Mount Sinai; we have obtained mercy and have full access to God and His dwelling. Jesus has forged the new covenant now and forever.

The people of Zion have not come to a mountain that cannot be touched, but have come to Mount Zion. To the myriads of angels in joyful assembly, to the congregation of the firstborn, enrolled in heaven. To God the Judge of all, to the spirits of the righteous made perfect, to Jesus the mediator of a new covenant, and to the sprinkled blood that speaks a better word than the blood of Abel. (Hebrews 12)

ZION'S DELIVERANCE

"Even the captives of the mighty man will be taken away, and the prey of the tyrant will be rescued; For I will contend with the one who contends with you, and I will save your sons." (Isaiah 49:25)

In Isaiah 49, the New Covenant promise is prophesied to Zion, proclaiming that the Lord will lift up His hand to the nations and set His standard, which is Jesus Christ, among the people, and deliver their children from captivity. The children of Zion will be liberated and established on the standard of the righteousness of Jesus and the sevenfold spirit of God brought forth through them.

The sevenfold spirit of God is described in Isaiah 11— the Spirit of the Lord, the Spirit of wisdom and understanding, the Spirit of counsel and might, the Spirit of knowledge, and the fear of the LORD. Also referenced in Revelation 4 as the seven lamps of fire before the throne of God, which burn as a torch.

The Zion children are the anointed and appointed remnant called to worship Him who sits on the throne, just as the twenty-four elders and the four living creatures worship Him and never cease to sing, "Holy, holy, holy, is the Lord God Almighty, who was and is and is to come!" They long for the complete essence of His name and the nature of His sevenfold spirit so as to establish themselves wholly in Him. The Lord is jealous for the seed of destiny within them; they are the chosen sons of Zion, and He will deliver them. He calls to them like deep calls unto deep, responding to their reverence, for they revere Him with throne room adoration.

THE HOLY CITY

"The Lord has chosen Zion; He has desired it for His dwelling place." (Psalm 132:11)

After a thousand years in Eden, the Book of Life is opened, and the dead are judged according to their deeds. The Lord brings destruction on all things evil and blesses the righteous, revealing a new heaven and a new earth, and the old will pass away. The holy city, which is Zion, filled with all whose names are written in the Lamb's book of Life, will come out of heaven from God, prepared as a bride adorned for her husband, shining radiantly in the glory of God, and she will be the Wife of the Lamb.

Zion is that holy city in God's future Kingdom when the consummation of all that God has willed has come to pass, comprised of all the remnant of all the ages who will be unified as one holy city, shining radiantly in the glory of God, as He inhabits our praise and we become His dwelling place.

CHAPTER 4

To be adequately prepared for the last days, it is necessary that we have (at least) a working knowledge of the Days of Noah.

~Paul Keith Davis

THE BLOOD CRIES

The final generation carries a unique gift for the transition of the ages. We will reap what was sown by the saints of old and will, by grace, freely receive the reward for the labor of all the previous generations. This is the end of the age revival, when the glory love of God is manifest. It is the recompense for the blood of Abel, the blood of martyrs, the blood of the innocent—the blood of every child sacrificed, and the blood of all the prophets.

The blood of the innocent cries out just as Abel's blood cries out. After Cain killed Abel, the Lord said to Cain, "What have you done? The voice of your brother's blood cries out to Me from the ground." This word for "cries out" means "summons, appeals as though for justice." Abel's blood will be restored by God's justice, and all the blood of all the innocent for every generation.

We are facing an evil that no prior age has faced. The battle over our destiny is intensifying, and the devil continues to oppose the eternal purpose of God's children. A bloodline war is in our midst, but God has remembered and will deliver our sons and fulfill His New Covenant promises. He will break the power of bloodline curses from generations of iniquity.

Acts of wickedness have remained in the shadows for far too long and are now being exposed. Nothing is concealed that will not become evident, nor anything hidden that will not be known and come to light. (Luke 8:17) What is being revealed by God will not always be easy for us to manage. God's unveiling of truth includes both wondrous mysteries from the heart of God and unsettling exposures of the enemy's wickedness.

The church must take courage as truth is revealed. These are dark times and impossible situations, but God will deliver His children. They are His heritage, and He will redeem. Many of the situations exposed by God are difficult to fathom, but the time has come to stand up for the children of this generation and every generation.

VAMPIRISM

An evil Luciferian energy is becoming increasingly rampant as we enter the latter stages of the end times. This is a phenomenon that much of the church has been unwilling to acknowledge. The Lord is exposing this sinister agenda. The enemy aims to empower his name by violating human life. This has always been the case since the beginning of time and has gained power and momentum. The enemies of God are feeding on the vital essence of humankind and vampirizing the children of God.

Predators are not only draining emotional energy but stealing from the life energy of humankind, specifically the children.

They aim to capture the awareness and essence of the child or adult and turn the human being into a sacrifice for selfish gain. They are driven by avarice, fame, and the desire for unparalleled supremacy, aiming to use any means possible to satisfy their insatiable appetite for power, even if it means stealing life from children through sacrifice and other means. The essence of a child is their life energy.

These iniquitous practices occur worldwide through satanic and religious ceremonies and by the global elite who understand that the power of life is in the blood, especially the blood of the innocent. They have been siphoning energy for their own benefit, ruthlessly exploiting and draining the vitality of humankind through the harvesting of the adrenalized blood of children and the manipulation of blood, attempting to gain immortality, youthfulness, and self-glory. This is vampirism.

ALUKAH: THE PRINCIPALITY OF THE AGE

The Bible warns ambiguously about the vampire agenda. The truth has been hidden like a riddle in the Holy scriptures and is now being revealed to equip us and confirm the nature of the age. Proverbs 30:14 exposes the principality of this age, vampirism, and its relentless, insatiable greed.

"There is an age (revolution of time) whose teeth are like swords and his jaw teeth like knives, to devour the poor from the earth and the needy from among men. The leech has two daughters, *Give* and *Give*." (Proverbs 30:14)

The word *leech* in Proverbs 30 is the Hebrew word *Alukah*, which means *leech* or *to suck*, and is interpreted by many scholars as a *blood-lusting monster* or *vampire-like demon*. Alukah symbolizes the unquenchable appetite of a filthy age that fuels their own wants and fleshly desires by stealing the life out of the innocent.

Proverbs 30:15 continues:

"There are three things that never satisfy and four that never say, 'Enough." The grave, the barren womb, Earth, that is never satisfied with water, and the fire never says, "Enough."

This is a moral warning about the principality of this age; only the fear of the LORD can restrain the dark forces. A broader implication indicates Alukah's connection to the curse of death. This is evident in the references to the grave, the womb, the land, and eternal fire. Each description that is used, describing the four occurrences, reveals the greed of the leech to suck the life out of humanity and curse the land and the womb, and is the scheme of the enemy in the end of the age. This is further confirmed in Proverbs 27,

"Sheol (death) and Abaddon (destruction) are never satisfied, nor is a malicious man."

Indicating the grave's appetite is unending, and the covetousness of humankind knows no limit, especially in the age of destruction. Alukah is a principality that is operating through evil people to drain the life out of the innocent and curse the womb that bears the seed of the chosen generation.

The riddle in Proverbs 30 exposes the plan of the enemy to curse humanity to death and eternal fire. The principality is also described in 2 Timothy 3:

"But realize this, that in the last days difficult times will come. For people will be lovers of self, lovers of money, boastful, arrogant, slanderers, disobedient to parents, ungrateful, unholy, unloving, irreconcilable, malicious gossips, without self-control, brutal, haters of good, treacherous, reckless, conceited, lovers of pleasure rather than lovers of God, holding to a form of godliness although they have denied its power; avoid such people as these. For among them are those who slip into households and captivate weak women weighed down with sins, led on by various impulses, always learning and never able to come to the knowledge of the truth. Just as Jannes and Jambres opposed Moses, so these men also oppose the truth, men of depraved mind, worthless in regard to the faith. But they will not make further progress; for their foolishness will be obvious to all."

Alukah is *Vampirism*, and vampirism is the principality of the end of the age. Proverbs 30 clearly states that Alukah has two daughters. I would presume to say that those two daughters are the spirit and the entity that are mentioned in Revelation 6: Death and Hades. Revelation 6 describes the fourth seal being opened and the release of the pale horse rider, which is Death, and is followed by Hades. The power to kill with sword, famine, and pestilence has been given to Death and Hades (specifically in this final age), strongly resembling Proverbs 30, and the destruction caused by Alukah, which are famine, death, and the grave.

The scriptures clearly portray the destructive nature of the end times. Proverbs 30:14 begins with "There is an age whose teeth are like swords." The word *age* means *revolution of time* or *generation*, indicating an era where vampirism will be rampant and whose people are depraved—metaphorically signifying the destructive and devouring actions of the wicked generation.

BREAKING THE FANGS OF THE WICKED

There is an obscure passage in the book of Job that appears to be a cryptic message describing a vampire-like being. It is a predator with serrated teeth that Job had to pry off his victim. For some context: Job is describing his favor with God when His lamp shone over his head and the friendship of God was over his tent. He expresses what he saw in the darkness and the righteous deeds he performed when He walked by God's light through the darkness. By God's light, Job delivered the afflicted and helped the poor. (Job 29).

The passage continues that during the peak of Job's favor, he investigates a case that he was not aware of. Job then describes rescuing the needy from an unrighteous and wicked enemy. It is worth noting that the peculiar description of the predator in this verse is not solely a metaphor, but an actual event, describing spiritual entities that have afflicted people for ages.

Job 29:17 says,

"I was a father to the poor, and I searched out the case that I did not know. Broke the fangs of the wicked and plucked the victim from his teeth."

RETRIBUTIVE PUNISHMENT

God is unveiling generations of deep corruption inflicted upon His children and will restore all that was stolen and bring retributive justice to their oppressors. He judges the wicked according to their way and according to what they deserve. (Ezekiel 7:27) The severity of divine consequences in the scriptures can reveal the underlying wickedness of an act, even when the act itself is not plainly described. We understand the nature of the sin committed based on the severity of the punishment. The punishment will fit the crime.

Isaiah 49 records the Word of the Lord and the retributive punishment for the enemy for the acts committed against the Sons of Zion:

"I will feed your oppressors with their own flesh, and they will become drunk with their own blood as with sweet wine; And all flesh will know that I, the Lord, am your savior and your Redeemer, the Mighty One of Jacob." Isaiah 49:26

Some scholars believe that this language implies internal strife amongst the enemy. This description is incomplete. If we take the principle of Ezekiel 7:27, "According to their conduct I will deal with them." The punishment against the enemies of Zion in Isaiah 49 is appropriate for someone who has committed crimes against the flesh and blood.

The word *flesh* is derived from the Hebrew word *basar*, which refers to the pudenda of a man, also referring to the body or genitals. The drinking of their own blood and eating of flesh/sexual organs indicate a fitting punishment for the violations that took place against the children of Zion, likely sexual acts and various blood crimes.

HYBRID RACE

The last days on earth are spiritually darker than any other age; abhorrent behavior, as it was in the Days of Noah, will be rampant across the Earth. Jesus said, "For as were the days of Noah so will be the coming of the Son of Man." In the days of Noah, angelic watchers left their habitation and cohabited with women, producing an offspring that the Bible describes as Nephilim. These were considered men of renowned for their extreme wickedness and disregard for human life. The last thing this hybrid race did before the flood was eat human flesh and drink human blood. This was to violate the laws of God as a final offense against God, leading up to the flood.

In many ways, the body of Christ has been very isolated and unwilling to believe the truth about this age and its present darkness. As the Lord reveals hidden truths, we are gaining understanding of the spiritual dynamics and the level of wickedness on the earth today. The revelation is appalling. However, we cannot hide from the truth even if we feel our hearts will fail us. The blood of millions of God's children cries out from the ground.

CHAPTER 5

The descent to hell is easy and those who begin by worshipping power, soon worship evil.

~C. S. Lewis

LUCIFERIAN ENERGY

The Lord is rescuing the children of this age, whom He has called into Light. He is delivering them out of gross darkness and away from the iniquitous practices of this evil age. The inner workings of darkness are, at the core, Luciferian and fuel Luciferian energy. Lucifer was intent on raising his throne above God's throne to glorify himself. Originally, Lucifer was a shining star who was given the Earth as his domain. He dwelt on the mountain of the Lord. He became proud and sinful and vowed to ascend to heaven and make himself like the Most High.

Ezekiel 28 states that his heart was lifted up because of his beauty, and he corrupted his wisdom for the sake of splendor. The Lord cast him out of the mountain of God. Lucifer's agenda is to become all-powerful and all beautiful by defiling sanctuaries; thus, his energy is fueled by violating the innocent. The agenda to fuel Luciferian energy was not commonly discussed in previous eras, but it is being exposed in this hour.

The life of children is high commodity for the workers of wickedness who aim to empower Luciferian energy. Each child or human that is sacrificed fuels this energy. This is the prominent motivation behind human and child trafficking. Slavery and child abuse have gone on for ages. Experts have calculated that roughly 13 million Africans were captured and sold as slaves between the 15th and 19th centuries. Today, nearly 50 million people of all races are victims of trafficking worldwide at any given time. It's estimated that for every reported incident, two go unreported. Children make up a significant portion of this. As reported by multiple sources, 25% of all victims are children trafficked and held in forced servitude.

According to experts, including Childlight Global, who, as per Childlight.org, are devoted to shining a light on the hidden pandemic of child exploitation and abuse, there are 300 million child pornography victims worldwide per year, and 1 out of 11 men in the United States alone has engaged in online behaviors at some point in their lifetime that could be classified as online child sexual abuse offending. Sexual exploitation and abuse of children has become a multibillion-dollar global trade. The wicked agenda appears almost invincible and covers the world. It involves key power players in the government, education, religion, and society.

DEEP DARKNESS

Satanic cults are a fertile field for these underworld activities, which include child pornography, sexual abuse, blood crimes, DNA manipulation, blood siphoning, blood magic and divination, abortion, and human sacrifice. Satanic cultic practices and rituals activate and fuel Luciferian energy by acquiring energy through human blood. The goal is to extract the soul essence of an entity, specifically the essence of children.

They understand the life in blood and therefore perform grotesque blood crimes against humanity, explicitly targeting the purest blood, which is the blood of a child. The motivation is not solely for financial gain, but for power, beauty, longevity of life, and to stir and enable the dark world energies. Even to the slaughtering and sacrifice of their own firstborn to siphon his/her blood and energy. They groom their children to do the same, creating an intergenerational curse that perpetuates itself through their bloodline.

In many cases, they will eat the flesh of a child in an attempt to acquire their IQ, enabling themselves to become all-knowing, comparable to Eve in the original garden, who was lured by Lucifer to eat of the tree of the knowledge of good and evil to become all-knowing. Lucifer's agenda continues through these wicked practices to defile sanctuaries for his own power, just as he did in the garden in the beginning.

SRA

Occultic practices and satanic ritual abuse are not only occurring in hidden ceremonies but are also demonstrated and live-streamed through social media, Hollywood, and music concerts. Many young people are exposed to these demonic art forms and are victimized through language and subtle symbolism. At times, concert performances are rituals under the misleading guise of artistic expression and are dedicated to Satan to gain greater authority in realms of darkness.

In 2021, a rapper, Travis Scott, performed a satanic ritual in concert on his Astroworld Tour with over 50,000 people in attendance. Fire filled the stage, vile symbols and satanic gestures, with a circular shape resembling a demonic portal. The rapper reportedly reached a frequency in sound that caused the audience to become ill, experience seizures, pass out, and lose their breath. The crowd began surging during this performance, causing a stampede that led to ten deaths, including a 9-year-old child. Witnesses claimed they had entered a demonic realm and felt hell surround them.

In 2023, the same artist was in Rome, Italy, performing for a crowd of over 60,000. He began singing a hit song "Fein," a play off of the word *fiend*, which means *the devil* or *spirit demon*, and is commonly used to describe vampires. The Luciferian energy in the crowd grew. Travis Scott quoted, "I go off the energy they give me." He played the song 10 times in a row, which eventually led to a documented 1.3 earthquake. A crowd of 60,000 people was enabling the dark world powers worshipping the devil; many of them were completely unaware of the level of darkness they were involved in. The workers of iniquity, however, know precisely what they are doing as they promote the principality of the age and prepare the atmosphere for the anti-Christ, fueling the Luciferian agenda.

A DARK BAPTISM

There are thousands of Satanic Ritual Abuse victims worldwide. Satanic victimization is not a fallacy. Luciferian energy is fueled through many different forms of abuse. In most cases, the victims' voices are never heard. Their blood cries out for victory. There are many recorded cases from survivors. Often, those cases are dismissed or written off as mental illness.

I sat with a girl many years ago as she shared her experience and the abuse she endured by these wicked forces. As a young teenager, she had a difficult and empty life. While longing for connection, she found false solace in a satanic group. She was eventually baptized in water in a satanic ritual. As she went under, she was overcome by dark energy forces. Coming out of the water, she recognized her soul was drastically different, and extreme torment began.

She was later diagnosed with "schizophrenia" and eventually pursued a life of constant drug use and self-harm. After years of treatment and counseling, she is finding stability in the love of God. Perhaps one day her mind will be entirely sound, but for now, she battles the memories and wicked energies.

I sat with her for hours as she explained the deep darkness that filled her during this ritual. I understand that deep, dark energy consumed her and began eating her spirit and soul. She was a young and impressionable teenage girl whose mind was overtaken by wicked forces.

IGNORANCE

The evidence of SRA is overwhelming, and still, many people have refused to accept the validity of the victims' stories. Here are a few testimonies of SRA which were recorded by professional psychologists, psychiatrists, law enforcement, and Christian leaders:

A teenage girl is impregnated during a satanic ritual, is forced to deliver her nearly term baby, and then is made to ritually kill the child and eat its heart as cult members watch. Another girl, a young child, is sewn inside the cavity of a disemboweled animal and rebirthed in ceremony. A preschool class is systematically abused by satanic pedophiles and pornographers. A young girl is thrown into an electric cage with wolves and ritually tortured to produce a wolf personality.

These diabolical events were disclosed in an article from the Christian Research Institute, attempting to disprove the validity of Satanic Ritual Abuse. Apparently, it was easier for the authors of this article to reject the notion that SRA victims are telling the truth, and that this vile behavior is even possible through humankind. Each memory surfaced when the victims were in a safe environment that allowed them to explore the painful memories. The details were brought to light so that healing could come. The authors of the article called the events "fallacies" and completely disregarded the victims' stories, even though professionals had validated their words and experiences.

For many years, the church has hidden from the deep darkness that has infiltrated every culture of the world. It has been easier to hide from reality than to face it. There is a deep, dark society and a Luciferian agenda that corrupts the earth and the church. It will intensify. A bloodline war is in our midst; the blood of humanity has been sought after in a cruel attempt to fuel the dark powers. We can no longer remain in ignorance. Those who stay in the darkness unknowingly fuel it by pretending it isn't happening. As it is brought into the light, it begins to lose its power.

As Christians, we believe that God sent His Son to die on the cross. He was persecuted, beaten, scourged, and crucified. The death and resurrection of God is the basis of Christianity. We believe and teach that evil men beat and murdered the Messiah, and by His shed blood, we are saved and have access to the Father. Yet many Christians are in denial about the true state of corruption in the world today. It is plainly stated in multiple verses throughout the Bible that the world will grow darker. 2 Timothy 3 states that those who desire to live godly in Christ will be persecuted (as Christ was persecuted) and that evil men and impostors will proceed from bad to worse. Is there a scenario more wicked than the murder of our Messiah? Yet the bible warns of deeper corruption. We cannot escape the reality of this evil age, nor hide in ignorance.

DARKNESS

Child sacrifice has embedded itself within traditional customs. Many children are sacrificed in their own homes by selfish parents through neglect, slavery, and mental and emotional abuse. This is a form of darkness. Child sacrifices through Satanic rituals, mutilation, sexual abuse, child trafficking, blood harvesting, and abortion are forms of deepest darkness. The enemy has ruthlessly attacked the innocent through all levels of cruelty.

Isaiah 60:2 says,

"For behold, darkness will cover the earth and deep darkness the people; But the Lord will rise upon you and His glory will appear upon you."

The verse presents two distinct categories: darkness and deep darkness. Darkness is miserable and sorrowful and includes death. Deep darkness is the most destructive form of darkness, referring to a thick gloom and severe cruelty. It originates from the root word *araph*, which means to decapitate or break the neck. Ignorance is a form of being in the dark. The Lord is highlighting the difference in cruelty yet shining His Light on all things, urging recognition that even unconscious engagement with darkness of any kind, even ignorance, fuels and empowers the dark world energies.

In ignorance, many unknowingly contribute to the intensification of the Luciferian energy by agreeing with perverse social agendas. Such agendas include but are not limited to abortion, corrupt vaccines, and religious cultism. Previous eras have not recognized the level of corruption within these practices. They are not simply political battles over ideals or framework for how the world and society should be structured. These are acts of wickedness. Any alignment, even in ignorance, empowers this force.

There are at least 45,000 denominations globally. Each denomination has its own religious protocols and culture. Often, they are not cultivating a spirit of love, selflessness, or true worship of God. On the contrary, many denominational churches promote selfish ambition and idolatry and are motivated by human zeal or religious protocol. Many well-meaning believers invest in religious systems and fruitless traditions of man. These systems are not motivated by the Holy Spirit and do not align with the heart of God.

In many cases, they do not glorify God but instead, empower the antichrist system and aim to energize the devil himself. False prophets and corrupt leaders have been given the platform, performing false signs and wonders, and leading many astray. (Matthew 24) This will continue to increase as wickedness increases. The souls of many people will become hardened and cold. All of these are motivated by the Luciferian agenda, and any cooperation with these dark forces inevitably amplifies their impact.

Traditions of the church, self-rule, and man-pleasing are clear forms of idolatry and are often done in ignorance by well-meaning people. In the past, God overlooked ignorance, but now he commands all people everywhere to repent. (Acts 17:30) As we approach the transition of the ages, all things will be exposed, and still deception will be rampant. The righteousness of God will increase in all who repent as the Spirit of Truth leads, and those who previously walked in ignorance or deception will instead revere His name and come to know the true knowledge of God.

CHAPTER 6

He purposed to show forth through man His dominion and power. This desire of God met with frustration in the Garden of Eden, when the creatures designed for His glory became the instruments of disobedience and shame.

~Frances Metcalfe

SEDUCTION AND THE TREE OF SELF-RULE

The story of Adam and Eve in the Garden of Eden is one of the most recognized and often recited biblical events. In this narrative, you will discover the Serpent who tempted Eve into participating in sin and eating from the Tree of Knowledge of good and evil. Ultimately, resulting in the fall of humanity and Adam's banishment from the Garden of Eden, and his access to the Tree of Life.

The original sin in the Garden of Eden was not the result of human frailty but was driven by the appetite for human self-rule. The tree of the knowledge of good and evil is a wicked portal and energy source. Everything that fuels the Luciferian energy in this age was in the tree of the knowledge of good and evil in the original garden. Eve violated the Earth and humanity when she transgressed the boundaries of God.

"But the fruit of the tree, which is in the midst of the garden, God has said, 'You shall not eat it, nor shall you touch it, lest you die." Then the serpent said to the woman, "You will not surely die. For God knows that in the day you eat of it, your eyes will be opened, and you will be like God, knowing good and evil. So, when the woman saw that the tree was good for food, that it was pleasant to the eyes, and a tree desirable to make one wise, she took of its fruit and ate. She also gave to her husband, and he ate." (Genesis 3:3-6)

She came into union with the knowledge of the evil one, consuming the reward of the tree of the knowledge of good and evil. She energized herself through the tree and claimed the fruit (reward) for her connection with the serpent. Eating of the tree of the knowledge of good and evil was not simply eating a piece of fruit. Eve was drawing from darkness and deep darkness to satisfy her sensuality and desire to be all-knowing and like God. She came into union with the beast and fueled Luciferian energy.

Fruit is a word that means *reward.* "You shall not eat, nor shall you touch." The word *eat* means lived off, devoured, consumed. *To touch* means to join, to agree with one, to draw near, to lay the hand upon, and can refer to lying with a woman. The enemy deceived Eve through sensuality. Eve interacted with the serpent, fueled the Luciferian energy, and was separated from God.

The true nature of the original sin has been veiled by ignorance throughout the ages, which has prevented the Church from operating in true authority. The urge to please the soul and satisfy the senses has kept many from their true calling in Christ, as they continue to draw from unclean sources to fuel their wants. The final, righteous generation understands the harsh reality of original Eden and is able to overcome the temptations that led Eve to be banished from the garden.

The tree of the knowledge of good and evil was appealing to the natural senses through counterfeit enlightenment. Natural senses are gateways to the soul and require constant guarding as we learn to train them to distinguish between good and evil. Eve did not guard her soul when she was seduced in the garden to yield to her own sensuality and disobey God's rule. This disobedience led to the corruption of her soul. Our senses, when sanctified by the blood of Jesus and guarded by reverential awe, will cooperate with our spirit man for true enlightenment, which is in Christ. This is what was available in the Tree of Life in the garden and is accessible to us by His great name.

BEGUILED

The interaction in the garden is more complex than we have been taught. Paul Keith expounds on this revelation and shares perspective about original sin and the seduction of Eve.

"Traditionally, the Serpent has been viewed as a reptile-like creature of deceit and temptation. However, the biblical narrative presents more to the story. We are introduced to the Serpent in Genesis 3:1 with the Hebrew word *nachash*. This word is typically translated as serpent, yet the Hebrew language, in its complexities, implies a divine being or one who practices enchantment. This dual meaning opens the door to a broader explanation of the serpent. A supernatural being with mystical knowledge and power.

It is also representing metaphorically a force of chaos or a rebellious divine being. In either event, he represents a rebel opposed to the purposes of God. He is both the tempter and one promising enlightenment.

Throughout ancient Mesopotamian culture and literature, the serpent is consistently represented as a symbol of deceit, perceived power, and knowledge. This implies that Eve's temptation was not merely an act of deception, but also an interaction that accessed divine knowledge and an act of human free will.

The serpent's promise of enlightenment aligns with the enemy of God, bringing knowledge to humanity. It reiterates the serpent's encouragement of the pursuit of wisdom and self-awareness, as well as a challenge to God's established order. It highlights the tension between God's ultimate authority and the quest for human enlightenment.

In the apostle Paul's epistle to the Corinthian church, he reiterates his devotion to the Lord's bride and his desire to present her as a "chaste virgin" to the Lord. Meaning that she had not been touched by the hands of men. In this New Testament typology, he is comparing the Lord's bride to Eve, who had been "beguiled/ seduced" by the serpent. This is no doubt very provocative language that lets us know much more went on in the Garden of Eden than many may suppose.

In the Old Testament passage, the word *beguiled* is taken from the Hebrew word *nasha*, meaning— to lead astray, to delude, or to morally seduce. In each biblical text where this word is used, it clearly implies to charm, enchant, deceive, or trick. This is the ploy used by the enemy to entice Eve to partake of the Tree of the Knowledge of Good and Evil.

Interestingly, following Adam's participation and the sin that resulted, they discovered their nakedness and experienced shame for the first time ever. In order to cover their shame, they took leaves to make aprons. When the Lord came into the garden, He instituted the need for blood to cover sin, not the produce of the ground. Something had to give its life to cover the shame of sin.

We see this further illustrated when both Cain and Abel offered their sacrifices to God. Cain from the fruit of the ground that he had labored to produce, while Abel sacrificed a lamb and shed his blood for the offering to God. The Lord had regard for Abel's offering but rejected Cain's. Abel was the first prophet and realized, by revelation, that it was blood that was commensurate with sin. Something had to offer its life to cover sin. The issue was blood."

When we return to the garden, the enemy will be bound, and the garden will be free from deception for one thousand years. The restored garden is absent of pain, disease, sorrow, debauchery, blood crimes, and wickedness. Still, rebellious people live in the land, but they do not act in wickedness because the energy of God restrains them.

At the end of the millennium, the enemy will again be released, at which time deception fills a multitude of people who have a rebellious seed. The enemy will gather them for a final rebellion against God, and they will come up on the broad plain of the earth and surround the camp of the saints and the beloved city. Then those who rebelled will all be consumed by the fire of God. Those who have the seed of the Father in heaven will not rebel and are never again deceived. They are the ones whose names are written in the Lamb's book of Life.

CHAPTER 7

"There is no peace for the wicked," says the LORD."

Isaiah 48:22

THE FOURTH SEAL

When *the Lamb* broke the fourth seal, I heard the voice of the fourth living creature saying, "Come!" I looked, and behold, an ashen horse; and the one who sat on it had the name Death, and Hades was following with him. Authority was given to them over a fourth of the earth, to kill with sword, and famine, and plague, and by the wild animals of the earth. (Revelation 6)

We are living in the Age of the Fourth Seal. The Fourth Seal has been opened, and the Pale (Ashen) Horse Rider has been released, and Hades follows. Authority has been given to them to kill the land and ultimately one-fourth of the earth's population. As mentioned previously, Death and Hades are connected to the principality of this age *Alukah*, which kills the soul by draining life through the siphoning of blood, energy, emotions, innocence, personality, and even IQ.

The Pale Horse Rider is death. The word *death* is the Greek word *thánatos* (derived from 2348 */thnḗskō), to die,* describing a physical or spiritual death. It is the separation from the life salvation of God forever by dying without first experiencing death to self to receive His gift of salvation. Ultimately, everlasting separation from God.

Death is followed by Hades. Hades is more than a place for departed souls. It is a separation from God and a place of incarceration for the wicked. While Death is to be separated, Hades is a holding place for the unrighteous dead who are separated from God, and it is the imprisonment for all the wicked awaiting God's judgment. Hades holds the unrighteous dead, and Heaven is a glorious holding place for the righteous who await the next phase of their eternal purpose, which is the resurrection of the dead, when the dead in Christ are risen at the catching away.

THE PALE HORSE RIDER

The end of the 19th century witnessed a significant spiritual shift that transitioned the church into an end-of-the-age prophetic perspective. This shift came with the impartation of the Flying Eagle anointing to overcome the pale horse rider of the fourth seal, which is the spirit of death.

In 1885, a conference was held in London, England, known as the Bethshan Conference on Holiness and Healing. 2000+ ministry leaders converged in London to explore the biblical affirmation of personal sanctification and physical healing as part of our redemptive privilege. In 1896, the commissioning of Alexander Dowie's Apostolic Church was an extension of this. From this community emerged many of the key figures that would form the perspective of early 20th-century Christianity. Men such as John G. Lake, Raymond T. Ritchie, Gordon Lindsay, and others. This led to the notable Welsh revival, followed by the Azusa Street revival, which introduced very significant expressions of outpouring, giving rise to a renewed understanding of New Testament Christianity. Modern Pentecost was born.

As the move of God's Spirit occurred, there was likewise an escalation among the realms of darkness. In the same timeline as these revivals, sinister members of the Luciferian order emerged, one such member was Aleister Crowley. Crowley was instrumental in the early part of the 20th century in pursuing occult activities and opening demonic portals. He attempted to harness power from the pyramid of Giza during the same time frame that revivalists were arising to power in God. During Crowley's attempts, members of the Luciferian order emerged, including various ancient Egyptian entities of darkness. This was the beginning of the release of the fourth seal and the pale horse rider.

The pale horse rider is the fourth level or stage of the maturity of the anti-Christ spirit. The opening of the fourth seal in the age of Laodicea occurred in part due to the summoning of demons, sacrifices, opening of portals, and satanic ceremonies performed by Crowley and others with the ultimate purpose to usher in the anti-Christ.

Although our desire is for these wicked events, such as the opening of the Fourth Seal, to be averted, the Bible has clearly prophesied that darkness will cover the earth, and deep darkness will fall upon the people. The release of the fourth seal contributes to the darkness of the age and the rise of the anti-Christ. Revelation 6:8 says, "Authority was given to Death and Hades to kill over a fourth of the earth with sword, famine, and pestilence, and by the wild beasts of the earth." The Lord oversees all things, and nothing takes place without His knowledge. The Pale Horse Rider was given authority; however, Crowley and others were also working with the dark world orders for the anti-Christ agenda by summoning the demonic realm to influence the release of death and Hades on the earth.

In a recent encounter, I was taken inside the fourth seal. I saw both the righteous and unrighteous who have died and will die in this era by the spirit of death, which is the spirit of this age. In this dream encounter, I saw Aleister Crowley and was told that he was a major contributor to the forming and conjuring of the Pale Horse Rider through the fourth seal. Aleister Crowley died in 1947.

By 1946, the stage was set for another major shift that identifies current spiritual conditions. On May 7, 1946, William Branham experienced an angelic visitation that commissioned him to carry the gospel of healing to the nations of the earth. Many other healing revivalists followed. Furthermore, the following years witnessed the extraordinary fulfillment of biblical prophecy as Israel was reborn as a nation on May 14, 1948. The discovery of the Dead Sea Scrolls in 1947 and 1948 provided key markers that offer a clear indication of first-century Christian literature and its present-day relevance in biblical prophecy.

Concurrently, key figures such as Jack Parsons and L. Ron Hubbard, under the tutelage of Aleister Crowley, pursued a project to open a demonic portal. They called it Babalon Working, with the sinister intent to incarnate the Thelemic goddess Babalon into a human woman. According to many prominent Christian leaders of the time (including Chuck Missler) they were successful in opening a demonic portal in April 1946. The stage was set for Isaiah's prophecy to be fulfilled. Darkness was covering the earth, and deep darkness the people; thus, the fourth seal continued to intensify.

Since the release of the Pale Horse Rider, more than 20 million people died in World War I, and more than 80 million in World War II, followed by over 70 million abortions globally per year and countless numbers of all-time abortions. Additional wars, murders, illnesses, viruses, vaccines, and pandemic deaths add to the number by the hundreds of millions, which will increase the closer we get to the Lord's return and into the great tribulation and wrath of God.

As the fourth seal intensifies and the wickedness of the final days increases, Christians mustn't energize the Luciferian powers and dark world orders either intentionally or in ignorance, so as not to partner with the development of the anti-Christ agenda.

The sons of God are given the authority to overcome the Pale Horse Rider. The Flying Eagle anointing has been given to those who will overcome the spirit of the age to soar, with His glory above the conflict of the land and the realms of darkness that have been released. It is imperative that we understand the culture of our time and the spiritual entities we face in this hour, so that we overcome. Those who overcome by the blood of the Lamb and the word of their testimony will inherit everlasting life and fulfill their eternal purpose in the Lord.

BROUGHT INTO HELL

We live in an age of lawlessness when death is rampant. Death is the spirit of the age, and it increases as we get closer to the end. Hades is an entity and a realm that appears to have many different intensities of darkness and despair. Several years ago, the Lord brought me, in the realm of the spirit, to see and experience Hades, which I experienced with all of my natural senses. I could not handle it for long; however, I knew the Lord required me to witness this dimension.

Evil, blackness, and utter despair consumed the atmosphere around; the feeling of suffocation intensified with each level. I was carried through space, hovering over the ground as a disembodied observer. While not truly present in Hell, the torment and emotions resonated deeply as though I was. I passed through a room and down a giant, enclosed steel box, similar to an elevator shaft, which lost oxygen the deeper it went into the center of the earth. Bugs, beasts, wicked entities, demons, and vile creatures of all kinds crawled from every crevice and intensified with each level.

Loneliness increased, and I was screaming for God to rescue me. This place is absent of God and all things good, but certainly God would deliver me from the belly of despair since He had brought me here to be witness to this place. The wicked beasts, though wretched, weren't as tormenting as the loneliness, shame, and utter anguish.

God eventually pulled me out of there. I felt each level of pain and evil peel off from me as I exited. By God's guidance, I was sucked backwards through the same shaft I had entered and out the door. Hell is beyond a grave for departed souls. It is separation and loneliness. Had I gone into deeper darkness, I presume there would be severe lashings and punishment suitable for every evil-willed soul.

God, in His graciousness, brought me away from that wicked realm, which was Hades, consumed of death, and separation, and into a delightful heavenly realm high in the sky, a dimension where God's presence was tangible. I understood that I was brought into the intimacy room of the Lord. There is an immeasurable disparity between the confinement and isolation in Hades and the vast realm of freedom and intimacy where God abides.

VARYING DEGREES OF THE UNDERWORLD

Hell, while not explicitly mentioned in the Bible, is an English word used to describe a place of torment for the dead, specifically unrighteous souls. The Old English word *helle* (first attested around 725 AD) is a concealed underworld. *Hell* referred to as *Hades* in the New Testament, is a holding place for the wicked until the Book of Life is opened and the dead are judged. Hades is commonly used in New Testament scriptures to describe the wicked underworld; however, there are various other words used to describe the different dimensions within Hades. Each of these descriptions indicate there are different levels of punishment. It would not be a far stretch to presume there are multiple realms of Hades each suitable for the nature of the sins that are committed.

Jesus said, "For the Son of Man is going to come in the glory of His Father with His angels and will then repay every person according to their deeds." (Matthew 16:27) In the same way the righteous receive a glorified body, rewards, and crowns, so will the wicked who are judged receive bodies that match their capacity for torment relating to their specific judgment.

The punishment of God has different levels of severity, depending on the weight of the sin and according to God's standards. Those with greater knowledge will be judged more strictly. Jesus taught the disciples about the importance of readiness and preparedness for the coming of the Master. Peter asked Him if He was speaking to them or to everyone, and the Lord responded,

"Who then is the faithful and sensible steward whom his master will put in charge of his servants, to give them their rations at the proper time? Blessed is that slave whom his master finds so doing when he comes. Truly I say to you that he will put him in charge of all his possessions. But if that slave says in his heart, 'My master will take a long time to come,' and begins to beat the other slaves and to eat and drink and get drunk, then the master of that slave will come on a day that he does not expect, and at an hour that he does not know, and will cut him in two, and assign him a place with the unbelievers. And that slave who knew his master's will and did not get ready or act in accordance with his will, will receive many blows, but the one who did not know it, and committed acts deserving of a beating will receive only a few blows." (Luke 12)

Each act received condign punishment, some more severe than others. A few lashings, many lashings, and ultimate judgment. The lawless slave received the same retribution as the unbeliever, which, according to Jesus, is eternal fire. (Matthew 25) This is one of the many provocative parables of Jesus that encapsulate retributive justice and the varying degrees of punishment due to the wicked.

Peter expounds on this teaching in 2 Peter 2, as he describes the depravity of false teachers who will receive the wages of unrighteousness. They carouse in the daytime in their own deceptions, adulterous and accursed, enticing unstable souls. The wage for the unrighteous false teacher who leads the weak astray is the blackness of deep and gloomy darkness (Zophos).

Clearly, there are many different descriptions of Hades, with varying levels of deep darkness within and beneath each other. These levels include Zophos, Tartarus, and multiple abysses. An abyss is a deep and boundless pit. Tartarus is the Greek word tar-tar-o'-o and is considered the deepest abyss of Hades, a place of incarceration to await final judgment and eternal torment. It is referenced in the scripture as the location where the fallen angels are detained until the day of judgment.

"For if God did not spare angels when they sinned, but cast them into hell (Tartarus) and committed them to chains of gloomy darkness (Zophos) to be kept until the day of judgment." (2 Peter 2:4)

Jude also refers to a dark place beneath and among Zophos where the fallen angels are kept. Zophos is a realm of darkness so dense and foreboding that it is considered apocalyptic; a nether world bringing indescribable despair. Tartarus is the deepest Abyss, yet it is woven like a spider web in with the gloomy darkness of Zophos and the wickedness of every other level of Hades.

Despite the brutal truth, it is essential to have a clear understanding of Death and Hades, as well as the nature of the era in which we live. Our motivation is to call people out of the darkness of this world and into God's glorious light, so that they may be saved from eternal darkness. We would be amiss to teach only of eternal life and the glorious rewards. Jesus also warns of eternal fire. Even as the apostles expounded on the teachings of Jesus about eternal life, Hades, and Gehenna (eternal fire), it is time we lay hold of both the eternal purpose in God and eternal damnation so as not to lead anyone astray, but to enforce the teachings of Jesus.

THE BLOOD ON HIS GARMENTS

This is a hard truth, facing the rampant wickedness in our world, and even harder to imagine the punishment reserved for the unrighteous. God has made it abundantly clear in scripture that these are the darkest hours of mankind. As previously mentioned, the Fourth Seal has been opened and will span the duration of this age, continuing through to the end of the age when the Lord returns for the righteous.

Then, the anti-Christ will appear publicly; he will be the embodiment of all evil. Many will be deceived by him. Those who oppose Christ are also operating in the authority of the anti-

Christ spirit and will receive just punishment for their actions. The Lord will bring divine retribution. He will slay His enemies in a great battle that has been long prophesied in the scriptures. The Lord judges and makes war. His robe is dipped in the blood of His enemies and the enemies of the Israelites who are awakening to their Messiah. (Revelation 19)

Isaiah 63 says,

"Why is Your apparel red, and Your garments like one who treads in the winepress? I have trodden the winepress alone, and from the peoples no one was with Me. For I have trodden them in My anger and trampled them in My fury; Their blood is sprinkled upon My garments, and I have stained all My robes. For the day of vengeance is in My heart and the year of My redeemed has come."

Christ the King is Faithful and True. He will complete everything He promises to do, including retributive punishment for the wicked. He will overcome His enemies in a great war, and the blood on His garments is the blood of His enemies. He will call for the birds of the sky and the beasts of the field to assemble for His sacrificial meal, declaring, "You shall eat the flesh of the kings and drink the blood of the princes of the earth. You shall eat fat until you are full and drink blood until you are drunk at My sacrificial meal. You shall be filled at My table with horses, riders, and mighty men." (Ezekiel 39)

The enemies of God become sustenance for the birds and beasts at the end of the great war, who will eat the flesh and drink the blood of the wicked. The triumphant festival takes place after the battle (likely at the end of the Great Tribulation) and is a powerful portrayal and stark illustration of God's judgment and reckoning for the wicked who have vampiristically assaulted the children of God.

The principality of this age, Alukah, and the workers of iniquity that aim to fuel Luciferian energy by draining the life of God's children will be destroyed. The punishment will meet the crime. For ages, they have done unthinkable acts to the children of God, such as blood crimes, vampirism, sexual abuse, and cannibalism and will ultimately reap a just punishment when God slays them and calls for the birds and beasts to make a spectacle of their death by eating the flesh and drinking their blood.

THE LAST ENEMY

Death and Hades will unleash devastation ceaselessly throughout the Great Tribulation, continuing to kill until the Kingdom Age comes, and Satan is thrown into the bottomless pit. While Satan is imprisoned in the abyss, Death and Hades are withheld from touching the children of God.

The abyss is a bottomless chasm of hell, literally referred to as "the abode for demons," and "home for the leviathan." (Job 41) The abyss is distinguished from the Lake of Fire. It is more appropriately a boundless, dungeon-like holding space for evil with unfathomable depth over which no creature exercises authority. According to Revelation 20, Satan is bound for one thousand years, and the sons of God rule and reign in the restored garden. The Abyss that Satan is detained in is a part of Hades and will ultimately be swallowed up by the lake of fire.

At the end of the millennium, Satan is released. Upon Satan's unleashing, a vast multitude greater than the sand of the shore is deceived by the devil again. God destroys them, and Satan is thrown into Gehenna. Gehenna is eternal fire— the place of post-resurrection torment strictly referring to the everlasting abode of the unrighteous, unredeemed where they experience God's judgment.

The Book of Life is opened, and the dead are judged. Those whose names are not written in the Book of Life are also thrown into Gehenna. Finally, death and Hades are thrown in the eternal fire. Death is the last enemy to be destroyed after the anti-Christ, the false prophet, Satan, and all whose names are not written in the Book of Life.

We will see two paradigms at the end of the age: Lawlessness and Righteousness. Rebellious people will strive to become an embodiment of evil by fueling Luciferian energy and edifying the anti-Christ agenda. Ultimately, wickedness is destroyed, but not before many are deceived. The wicked will be rewarded with just punishment for their unrighteous acts. Conversely, the righteous sons of God will pursue God's nature and become the essence of His name, thus receiving various rewards based upon how they obeyed and pleased the Lord.

The stubborn and unrepentant heart is storing up wrath for itself, which will be in the day of wrath and of the revelation of the judgment of God, who renders to each according to his deeds. For the unrighteous, wrath, indignation, and ultimately, eternal fire (Gehenna). For those who obey and hold fast to the name of the Lord, His new name and eternal life. (Romans 2:5)

CHAPTER 8

Human believers in their final state are made like Jesus. We become fit for sacred space in the most ultimate way. We as human beings are created lesser than the Elohim. We are elevated to that position, that status rank, and form newly constituted counsel with God to enjoy creation and manage it. We will do whatever God wants done in the final state. God gets His way with a restored Eden, and we are His glorified family along with the members of the heavenly host who remain loyal to Him. We have a corporate family partnership model at the end of the days.

~Dr. Michael S. Heiser

BEYOND TIME

Though death is the culture of the world during these perilous times, the Spirit of Life dwells amidst the Sons of God. The Spirit of Life is unending; its purpose goes infinitely beyond the boundaries of time and space, as our story in Him is eternal. We have always been in the heart of God, destined beforehand according to His purpose (Ephesians 1). As Christ lives, so do we live, hidden away in God to be revealed with Christ in glory.

The Omega generation possesses an eternal vision, understanding their lives are a part of an enduring legacy of love and union in God. We have an infinite destiny beyond time, and what we do on earth matters and confirms our future position, which is not complete when our days as mortal men come to an end. Our eternal purpose spans even beyond 1,000 years in Eden, and there will be a new Heaven and a new Earth, and we will become as one in Him.

In preparation for His appearing, a remnant will become transparent, mystical men and women of spirit who operate from a realm of love that few have journeyed. We are preparing for a massive existence with the spirit family we have longed for and our inheritance in Him who is able to do exceedingly abundantly above all we ask or imagine. He is coming quickly, bringing His reward.

"Behold, I am coming quickly, says the Lord, 'My reward *is* with Me, to reward each one as his work deserves. I am the Alpha and the Omega, the first and the last, the beginning and the end." Revelation 22

WHEN JESUS COMES

The signs of the times confirm that His return is imminent, and with great expectation, we joyfully await His appearing and our bodily redemption in Christ. We have unwavering hope for the transfiguration and the translation of the living saints; when the trumpet sounds, the dead will be raised imperishable, and we will all be changed. The dead in Christ, who are the bride of the prior generations, will rise first. Then, those alive will be caught up, and all will meet the Lord in the air.

We do not know the amount of time between the rising of the dead and the catching away. During this time, Christ does not touch His feet to the earth. We are all ascended into marriage union and the marriage supper. After the completion of the marriage union and marriage supper, the Lord will return with His bride to the earth. At this time, the Lord will touch the earth on the Mount of Olives, and the mount will split in two; the geography of Jerusalem will be changed.

The Lord will deal with his enemies; the anti-Christ and the false prophet will be thrown into the lake of fire, and Satan will be bound in chains (by Michael) and thrown into the pit for one thousand years. At the end of the millennial reign, he, too, will be thrown into Gehenna for eternity.

RESTORING THE KINGDOM

During the thousand years, referred to as the Millennial Reign of Christ, those on earth will live in perfect cooperation and union with Him. It will be to their renown on the day He will show His glory. Those who have overcome the spirit of the last days and stand firm in Christ to the end will receive rewards from Him, including ruling and reigning with Him on His throne during the thousand years.

Eden will be rebuilt by His chosen ones who will wear out the work of their hands, restoring the land. (Isaiah 65) The people will tend to the earth as it is renewed from all that it will endure, even burying, for seven months, those who have died in wrath. They will build houses and inhabit them, plant vineyards and eat fruit, and ultimately enjoy the peace within creation as the wolf and the lamb graze together and creation praises God and reveals His glory.

This will be restored Eden in which our Messiah will rule planet Earth along with His bride. Much of the prophetic Scriptures throughout the Old Testament portray this epoch and its beauty, majesty, joy, and divine government. The Lord will express His righteous leadership for one prophetic day (one thousand years) to show humanity His invisible attributes, divine nature, and eternal power.

At the end of that age, there will then be the creation of a new heaven and a new earth, typified by the eighth day of the Feast of Tabernacles. This will be the age of infinity in which the elements will melt by fervent heat, and a new heaven and new earth created that will accommodate New Jerusalem.

THOSE WHO DIE AND THOSE WHO RISE

Omega time is the final span of time leading up to the catching away, the marriage union, the marriage supper of the Lamb, Eden, and beyond. The chosen people who have the seed of God and are called to live during Omega time are categorized into two distinct groups. One group will not taste death at all but will live through into the resurrection and the catching away. The other group will experience death and go to heaven, which is a holding place for the righteous who die in the Lord. Heaven is not our final destination; it is a holding place. Those who die in the Lord will be resurrected at the end of the age. They will be resurrected first with those from every age who died in Christ. Together, those who are resurrected from the dead and those who never died will be caught up together and meet the Lord in the air, and from that time on they will always be with Him.

"But we do not want you to be uninformed, brothers and sisters, about those who are asleep, so that you will not grieve as indeed the rest of mankind who have no hope. If we believe that Jesus died and rose from the dead, God will also bring with Him those who have fallen asleep through Jesus. For we say this to you by the word of the Lord, that we who are alive and remain until the coming of the Lord will not precede those who have fallen asleep. For the Lord Himself will descend from heaven with a shout, with the voice of the archangel, and with the trumpet of God, and the dead in Christ will rise first. Then we who are alive, who remain, will be caught up together with them in the clouds to meet the Lord in the air, and so we will always be with the Lord." (Thessalonians 4:13-17)

For those who die and those who rise, the ultimate purpose remains the same: Oneness and perfection for the age of infinity without the encumbrance of sorrow, woe, or separateness. The beauty of the promise of Thessalonians 4:17, "And so we will always be with the Lord," clearly portrays endless love in union with Him. There will still be work to be done in the garden, fields to tend and restore, and vineyards to build, yet we will do it all in perfect cooperation with Him whose yoke is easy and burden is light.

THE DEAD IN CHRIST

In the time of Omega, many people will go on to sleep (die) in the Lord. Those who will go home in Him will return when He returns. This is part of their calling. They must die in order to be resurrected from the dead when He returns, and the dead in Christ are risen first. They have a different calling than those who will live through the transition of the ages (from this age to the Kingdom age). Those who die will be a part of the resurrection at the end of the age. Until then, they will rest from their labor.

"Blessed are those who die in the Lord from now on. Yes, they are blessed indeed that they may rest from their labors, for their deeds follow them." (Revelation 14:13)

THE MARTYR'S FRAGRANCE

A symbol of honor is reserved for martyrs, willing to die for the sake of righteousness. God rewards each one according to their work and rewards the martyrs with a crown of life. The martyrs of all ages will attain to the resurrection from the dead, having become like Him in His death, and will receive the crown of life. Blessed is the man who endures temptation. He will receive this reward as promised by the Lord to those who love Him and are willing to die for righteousness' sake.

The message to the Smyrna church in Revelation 2 expresses this promise of the crown of life to the martyrs and reveals an attribute of the Lord that coincides with this reward, stating that the Lord is the first and the last who died and came to life. Those who willingly shared in Christ's sufferings and in His death will receive a victor's crown.

"To the angel of the church in Smyrna write: 'The words of the first and the last, who died and came to life.

"Do not fear what you are about to suffer. Behold, the devil is about to throw some of you into prison, that you may be tested, and for ten days you will have tribulation. Be faithful unto death, and I will give you the crown of life. He who has an ear, let him hear what the Spirit says to the churches. The one who conquers will not be hurt by the second death.'

The name Smyrna means "myrrh," an anointing oil and spice which was used to prepare the dead for burial. The martyrs of the Smyrna time period set a standard for future generations. They were crushed by the full fury of the Roman Empire, but the more they were killed, the more fragrant the aroma before God and men. Men marveled at their great courage and converted to Christ faster than Rome could kill them. The faithfulness of the martyrs released an aroma pleasing to God and recognizable to men. So shall there be a sound of gladness from the heavens for the martyrs of our day who have loved not their lives even unto death. (Paul Keith Davis)

OIL OF THE RESURRECTION

God raised Christ up on the third day and granted that He be revealed, not to all the people, but to witnesses who had been chosen beforehand by God. Likewise, He has chosen a people who will see the resurrection at the end of the age and be caught away with Him in the sky. They are destined to live through the transition of the ages. Death is not in their story.

The spirit of death will be in operation; however, those who are called to remain on the earth until that day will not die but will live. If the enemy kills them before their time, they will be raised immediately, often by those who carry resurrection power.

Those who are destined to live through the transition of the ages will be anointed with the oil of the resurrection. A specific allotment of favor is granted to them to operate in resurrection power, healing the sick, casting out demons, and raising the dead. They will be like Christ and will operate in realms of God's glory by the power of His name, amidst the angels, cooperating with the Holy Spirit for the perfecting of the bride.

Though death is the culture of the age, resurrection life is the culture of the kingdom of God. Those with a kingdom purpose understand resurrection power. What they touch comes to life. Curses are broken, including death. Jesus said, "I am the resurrection and the life. The one who believes in me will live, even though they die; and whoever lives by believing in me will never die." (John 11:25)

ANOINTING FOR A KING

In one of the most touching stories of scripture, Mary displays sacrificial devotion to Christ, anointing Him for burial with an entire bottle of her spikenard oil. Mary poured it on Jesus' feet and wiped His feet with her hair. And the house was filled with the fragrance of the perfume. In those days, spikenard oil was often given as an inheritance to young women. Quite likely, the oil she lavished upon Jesus was everything she had of worth in the world. She was prepared to give Him the most valuable item she owned. The perfume is a symbol of great sacrifice. She washed His feet with tears and spikenard in reverence for Him.

As others questioned her choice to use such expensive perfume, Jesus said of her, "It was intended that she should save this perfume for the day of my burial." (John 12:7)

Mary understood the existential role of the Messiah in His Alpha ministry (early ministry). Likewise, those intended for the end of the age will understand His Omega ministry and will sacrifice everything this world has to offer to be prepared for His return.

Embracing our divine calling in God means fully yielding to Him. Our overwhelming love for Him eclipses every struggle and every need in this world; He is our ultimate source who gives grace to those who humble themselves. We are overcoming temptation through our willingness to give everything over to Him, every element of this world that deters us from our purpose, which is for eternal life and union in Him. We are in the time of the end, and the spirit of death is rampant. The Lord has released a grace for those who surrender to their eternal purpose in Him, for some martyrdom and some deathlessness in Him, but to all resurrection power.

CHAPTER 9

"The Spirit and the bride say, "Come." And let the one who hears say, "Come." Revelation 22:12

DAUGHTERS OF SHILOH

A special holiday, referred to as Love Day (similar to Valentine's Day), is celebrated in Israel on the 15th day of Av, also known as Tu B'Av. The Tu B'Av celebration is a matchmaking festival where young men come to find potential wives among maidens. Historically, the maidens of the land who wish for marriage take this day to dance joyously in vineyards, in hope for a groom.

The festival of Tu B'Av originated with the tribe of Benjamin and is recorded in the Book of Judges. The tribe of Benjamin had acted wickedly. As a result, they were almost entirely decimated (similar to Sodom and Gomorrah). Several hundred Benjamites were left without partners for marriage because the women had been destroyed. The elders of the congregation said, "What shall we do for wives for those who remain since the women of Benjamin have been destroyed?" And they said, "There must be an inheritance for the survivors of Benjamin, that a tribe may not be destroyed from Israel." (Judges 21:17)

The Benjamites hoped for a patrimony, but the situation was further complicated due to the vow, "cursed be he who gives a wife to Benjamin." The other tribes repented of their anger and devised a plan for the Sons of Benjamin to be able to marry.

There was a yearly feast, and the women of Shiloh would come out in their dresses, dancing. The men of Benjamin were instructed to go lie in wait in the vineyards, and watch; and just when the daughters of Shiloh come out to perform their dances, they come out from the vineyards, and every man catches a wife for himself from the daughters of Shiloh. This marked the beginning of this historic ancient festival. To this day maidens dance in white gowns on Tu B'Av in a vineyard. They dance with joy, rejoicing over their future bridegroom.

The Sons of Benjamin and the Daughters of Shiloh modeled the scenario that will occur during the transition of the ages when the bridegroom snatches His bride for Himself. The dancing maidens of Judges 21 are considerably like the wise virgins mentioned in Matthew 25, who wait for their Bridegroom with oil in their lamp, knowing the bridegroom will come and are prepared for His coming. After the marriage supper, the Lord and His bride return to the earth to reign together in the Kingdom Age for one thousand years.

When the Kingdom era begins, we will work together to purify the land. The earth will have experienced extreme trauma, and God has prophesied the cleansing of the land that will take place.

"I will raise up its ruins and rebuild it as in the days of old... I will restore the captivity of My people Israel, and they will rebuild the ruined cities and live in them; They will also plant vineyards and drink their wine and make gardens and eat their fruit. I will plant them on their land, and they will not be rooted out from their land, which I have given them." Says the Lord your God."' Amos 9

The Benjamites chose their wives, then returned to their inheritance and rebuilt and inhabited the cities. The children of Israel departed at that time, each man to his own tribe and family, to experience their inheritance. It is plausible that we will work together to rebuild Eden in the same way the Benjamites and their wives rebuilt the cities after the destruction. We are responsible for restoring the earth and inhabiting the land. The house of Israel will bury the dead for seven months to cleanse the land. And all the people of the land will bury them; and it will be to their renown on the day that the Lord appears in glory. We will select men who will constantly pass through the land, burying those bodies remaining on the ground to cleanse it so that the land will not be defiled. The land will be brought to health and healing, and God will reveal to us the abundance of peace and truth. (Ezekiel 39)

The bride will experience our inheritance together with God in Eden. Unity with Him in the restored garden is a foretaste of our eternal union as New Jerusalem when God will dwell in His city forever. There is an eternal seed within us that is emerging in the true knowledge of God. Our inheritance is in the seed. As we come into union with God, our inheritance is opened to us. We will know union with Him and be purified vessels in whom He will abide. The power for eternal indwelling is in Jesus, who lives in God, and God lives in Him, and they are one. So will we be one. We have only experienced a morsel of what is available to us. This is our inheritance, to dwell with God and He in us. (1Peter 1:23)

JOY OF HIS APPEARING

The history of the Daughters of Shiloh is also a prophetic parable, describing the scenario when the Lord appears. Each maiden moved in joy and danced in love for their husband, expectant to be chosen to come away with him, longing joyfully for union with their lover. Likewise, the Beloved does not wait in hopelessness or sorrow; we joy at the revelation of His appearing and eagerly await our full inheritance, which is for God to inhabit us and dwell in our midst, and we in Him.

Christ entered heaven to appear in the presence of God on our behalf, having died, bearing the sins of many. He was offered once to bear the sins, and He will appear a second time, not to deal with sin but to save those who eagerly wait for Him. (Hebrews 9:28) The word *eagerly* is a word meaning *to expect fully* and *to put away all that should remain behind.* Many will not acknowledge the truth of His return, and as a result, they will miss the joy of His appearing. In Matthew 25, the foolish virgins were not prepared, and the door to the banqueting hall for the marriage feast was closed, and they were not permitted to enter. Those who wait for Him and endure to the end will experience the joy of His appearing.

"Finally, the crown of righteousness is laid up for me, which the Lord, the righteous Judge, will give to me on that Day, and not to me only but also to all who have loved His appearing." (2 Timothy 4:8)

INHERITANCE

Our inheritance is eternal, and we are emerging into our purpose in Him. Paul said, "For I consider that the sufferings of this present time are not worthy to be compared with the glory that is to be revealed to us. For the eagerly awaiting creation waits for the revealing of the sons and daughters of God."

He has sealed us and given us His Spirit which is a first installment of our inheritance and is a pledge in our hearts of what is to come (2 Corinthians 1:22). We have been given the first fruit of the Spirit, yet we are waiting eagerly for our adoption as sons and daughters, the redemption of our body. Though these blessings will be fully revealed in the Kingdom Age, the virtues are attainable now. By the spirit of wisdom and of revelation in knowledge of Him, we move deeper into His presence and access our inheritance, which includes mature sonship.

The book *Voice of the Bride (pg. 38-42)*, by Paul Keith Davis clearly lays out the fundamental teaching of the mystery of adoption and clarifies the inheritance available to us as mature sons of God. Although adoption is not the final expression of our life in Christ, it is the vital progression that moves us deeper into our eternal purpose.

"The spirit of adoption is a powerful spiritual impartation that provokes us from infancy into adulthood. Romans 8:14-15 declares:

"For all who are being led by the Spirit of God, these are sons *huious* of God. For you have not received a spirit of slavery leading to fear again, but you have received a spirit of adoption as sons by which we cry out, "Abba! Father!"

Just as there is the spirit of faith, the spirit of revelation, the spirit of healing, so also is there the spirit of adoption as a meaningful deposit of the Holy Spirit that moves us from immaturity into the place of adulthood. When the spirit of adoption comes upon us, it is an impartation of grace that takes us from where we are to where we need to be for our full inheritance to be released. It is a provocation to grow and progress into a mature man. It is a literal fulfillment of Hebrews 6:1-5, moving from the elementary principles into the fullness of maturity.

"Therefore, leaving the elementary teaching about the Christ, let us press on to maturity, not laying again a foundation of repentance from dead works and of faith toward God, of instruction about washings and laying on of hands, and the resurrection of the dead and eternal judgment. And this we will do, if God permits. For in the case of those who have once been enlightened and have tasted of the heavenly gift and have been made partakers of the Holy Spirit and have tasted the good word of God and the powers of the age to come."

In this passage, we see four distinct progressions.

1. Once enlightened, justification by faith
2. Tasted of the heavenly gift, sanctification by the washing of the water of the Word

3. Made partakers of the Holy Spirit, the baptism of the Holy Spirit
4. The tasting of the good Word of God and the powers of the age to come

It is this fourth and final progression that is of paramount importance as it relates to the mature sons of God in these last days. The model for what will be displayed in this hour cannot be found in the past but must be apprehended by revelation from the age to come. The mature sons who have experienced full adoption will demonstrate a first-fruits representation of the age to come. It will be an introduction to the new age as we culminate the present Church age. This is a fundamental aspect of the harvest.

The model for what will be displayed in this hour cannot be found in the past but must be apprehended by revelation from the age to come. It is believed by many scholars that the apostle Paul wrote the book of Romans from Corinth around 57 A.D. This would've been the end of Paul's third missionary journey. At the time, Rome was under the wicked leadership of Nero. Though the Church of Rome had been severely persecuted, it had persevered for many years with a strong core group of saints who were prepared to hear the deep truth that God revealed through Paul in this amazing epistle.

By the time Paul penned Romans, he had been serving the Lord as an apostle for nearly twenty-five years and had endured great hardship for the sake of the gospel. He had been imprisoned, stoned, beaten, shipwrecked, and persecuted; all this while birthing numerous churches and writing profound epistles concerning church order and the great revelations that had been entrusted to him.

Paul acknowledged that his revelation came not by the teaching of men nor by the reading of a book but by the revelation of Jesus Christ (Gal. 1:12). Clearly, by the time he wrote Romans 8, he was a seasoned believer walking with the Lord for a quarter century. With that brief background in mind, let us now examine Romans 8:22-23 to understand more fully Paul's perspective on adoption, saying:

"For we know that the whole creation groans and suffers the pains of childbirth together until now. And not only this, but also, we ourselves, having the first fruits of the Spirit, even we ourselves groan within ourselves, waiting eagerly for our adoption as sons, the redemption of our body. Notice how Paul includes himself in this passage as he writes to veteran believers who have paid a great price for their walk with God. These are not people seeking to become believers but those who have been serving the Lord for many years. They were sealed into God by the Holy Spirit and possessed the first fruits of the Spirit, including Paul himself. Yet he says,

"We ourselves groan within ourselves, waiting eagerly for our adoption as sons."

This is a profound passage as it relates to the truth of spiritual adoption. Paul was not looking to the past to reflect on his new birth experience, but rather looking to the future and his full adoption as a mature son with complete access to the fullness of his inheritance, including the redemption of His body. As such, no longer living according to the laws of sin and death but according to the laws of the Spirit of Life in Christ Jesus. Redemption means to put back in its original order. Death is the result of sin. Once full adoption has been experienced, the curse and effects of the laws of sin and death have been entirely broken, and the Spirit of Life prevails.

This places adoption as a last-day principle of the Spirit that must be understood for us to become the manifestation of God's sons who do the works Christ did and even greater works. Paul said he was groaning within himself, longing for his adoption. The word *groaning* is the Greek term *stenazo*, meaning "to sigh deep within, murmur or pray with groaning for something's reality." The very core of Paul's being cried out for his adoption (the setting in place) as a mature son. As we approach the end of this age, this truth will have even greater implications. The Bible tells us the end of the age is the harvest. The harvest implies that all things have come to maturity simultaneously. The sons of the Kingdom must come to a place of complete maturity to respond to the sons of the evil one as they come to the fullness of their maturity."

CHAPTER 10

The Bible is not an end in itself, but a means to bring men to an intimate and satisfying knowledge of God, that they may enter into Him, that they may delight in His Presence, may taste and know the inner sweetness of the very God Himself in the core and center of their hearts.

~ A. W. Tozer

THE COUNSEL OF HIS WILL

The Spirit searches all things, even the depths of God, and will reveal to us the things that are to come, including the hidden wisdom which God predestined before the ages to our glory. There are many passageways in His heart, and the depths of God span eternally in every direction. His formation is endless. The sound of God reverberates from every channel, and His Spirit brings forth the Word.

Each message is revealed by the Spirit and must pass through the counsel of God before it is released. The counsel of God is in the heart of God. The heart of God is a realm of ultimate rule, where mercy is the pulse beat and rhythm. He judges the world with righteousness according to His infinite power and rules the people with equity. He judges according to the rule of mercy.

Ultimate judgment rules over every prophetic promise that has been written and concealed in the scrolls of destiny. They are His own words created in His infinite wisdom, yet still, He chooses to rule and agree with His promises, confirming His work and ruling in agreement with His design. God recalls all of His creation, including His creative words, and says, "Behold, it is good." (Genesis 1:31)

Each promise comes before Him and is judged by rule of mercy. In this place of decision, He distinguishes each word of hope and every rebuke, bringing them into the counsel of His will. Before they are released, they are judged by rule of mercy that He might make known the riches of His glory on the vessels of mercy (Romans 9).

He makes known to us the mystery of his will, which he set forth in Christ as a plan for the fullness of time, to unite all things in Him, things in heaven and things on earth. Every created thing must confront the counsel of His will.

DIVINE COOPERATION

The Omega generation carries a message for the end of the age and for the transition of the ages. The Lord is bringing to light the secrets of His heart, which have been hidden for ages, reserved for this final generation. Things which eye has not seen, and ear has not heard, and which have not entered the human heart (1 Corinthians 12). He has orchestrated a divine plan to bring His Omega message, which involves a great cooperation of messengers of all kinds. The messengers of the Lord do His deeds, champion His heroes, and war on behalf of the Saints.

The Kingdom of Heaven is organized of many workers in all places of dominion who execute the Word of the Lord. The holy ones from the heavenly realm watch over the Word. They are the guardians. The angelic hosts of heaven perform His Word and carry it where it is intended. Humankind will speak the Word as it is awakened within, and they will parabolically experience the message to its fulfillment. Those previously called intercessors are more appropriately forerunners, who support the messenger and carry the word in prayer and supplication. In quietude, they engage the Mind of His Spirit to receive His words to pray. This is called Omega prayer. The words that are being released and activated in this hour are too large to carry alone. The Lord has orchestrated a divine cooperation.

There is divine order in the Kingdom of God, and His workers will not transgress against the order but move in the very structure of His Kingdom. He has established His throne in Heaven, and He is superior to every created thing. The Most High is ruler over the realm of mankind and bestows it on whomever He wishes, and has given the watchers in the heavens governing authority over certain areas. The realm of the spirit has a hierarchy that is constantly at work, battling for the full realization of each message, which will ultimately bring us into the unity of the faith and the True Knowledge of God.

A REALM OF WAR

The Mind of His Spirit is different from the realm of the spirit. The realm of the spirit is a realm of war, for warring over the promised Word. The word of God will accomplish the purpose for which He sent it, He has orchestrated a perfect cooperation of humankind and heavenly beings to achieve His intention.

The realm of the spirit consists of spiritual beings, both good and evil, who are in a constant battle. Demons, principalities, and rulers in dark places are continuously attempting to thwart God's promises and interrupt the release of God's words by destroying the people of God. God, who knows the end from the beginning, has put together a team to protect and administer His messages and, by His Spirit, secure His Word. According to Jeremiah 1:12, the Lord says, "I am watching over My Word to perform it."

We receive His word in the Mind of His Spirit and do not engage the spirit realm of our own accord. He sends his warring angels to battle on our behalf in the spirit realm. These two realms are greatly exemplified in Daniel 10. Daniel was shown a vision and given a message of the latter days. The message he received from God was about the final generation who will execute God's words in the final days (Omega time) before the Lord's appearing. While he was receiving the impartation, a war was occurring in the unseen realm.

"In the third year of Cyrus, king of Persia, the word was revealed to Daniel, and the word was true, and it was a great conflict." Daniel 10) Daniel understood the word and the vision. He had mourned and fasted for three weeks prior to receiving the message. He received a great vision and heard a powerful message; after seeing the vision, no strength was left in him. Upon hearing the voice of the messenger, he fell on his face in deep sleep with his face to the ground. At this time, the archangel spoke to Daniel, "O Daniel, man greatly loved (treasured), understand the words that I speak to you, and stand upright, for now I have been sent to you."

When he spoke, Daniel stood up, trembling. He said, "Daniel, fear not, for from the first day that you set your heart to understand and humbled yourself before your God, your words have been heard, and I have come because of your words. The prince of the kingdom of Persia withstood me for twenty-one days, but Michael, one of the chief princes, came to help me, for I was left there with the kings of Persia, and came to make you understand what is to happen to your people in the latter days. For the vision is for days yet to come." (Daniel 10)

The warrior angel, likely Gabriel, was delayed from reaching Daniel by a demonic entity, the prince of Persia. Michael intervened to help Gabriel overcome the demonic force and deliver the message to Daniel. The conflict between the archangels and the principalities of those regions (Prince of Persia and eventually Prince of Greece) occurred in the unseen realm of the spirit. It is the dimension of warfare, for warring over the promised word. Michael and Gabriel contended over the word to ensure its delivery to Daniel. Daniel is the prophetic messenger who carried the message in his heart and released the word in his writings. The Word of God is established in the mind of the Spirit.

The battle over Daniel's message continues in this age. Michael came at the end of the 21 days of Daniel's fast and has come for the end of the church age, to assist in the expression of this word through the Omega people, who have a pivotal role in the fulfillment of what was revealed to Daniel. He will war in the realm of the spirit alongside the angel armies who are under his hierarchy. They will battle against the principality of this age that resists the message. Michael will assist the Omega people and protect the word just as he was sent to do in Daniel 10.

MIND OF HIS SPIRIT

The unseen realm has spirits, both good and evil, but the mind of His Spirit is reserved for the sons of God. His thoughts and mysteries are hidden in him, and His Spirit searches everything, even the depths of God. The principalities of this age cannot discern His thoughts, for no one knows the thoughts of God except the Spirit of God.

The mind of His Spirit is not a dimension of conflict as is the spirit realm; The mind of His Spirit is life and peace where the promised Word is found. Romans 8:5-6 says,

"For those who are according to the flesh set their minds on the things of the flesh, but those who are according to the Spirit, the things of the Spirit. For the mind of the flesh is death, but the mind of the Spirit is life and peace."

The unseen realm is complex and convoluted by human emotions, self-focus, spiritual warfare, and demonic influence. The Mind of His Spirit is perfect and clear. Here we receive a pure Word from the heart of God, which shifts the entire atmosphere in one declaration. By rule of mercy, everything is transformed, as the word of God comes forth and judges the thoughts and intentions of the heart. In unfeigned delight, we align with His will and are moved deeper into union with Him.

CHAPTER 11

Let all the mystics return to the rhythm of our story- The story of eternal union. ~Amy

ENGAGEMENT WITH CHRIST

The Omega generation pursues a different model than previous generations, one established in the age to come and implemented on Earth. The understanding of our earthly purpose has been distorted due to human self-will, but is now being defined with more clarity than ever before. We are being drawn deeper into the heart of the Father to become like Him in integrity and character and to learn union with Him and our spirit family.

It is all-important to comprehend the characteristics of the end of the age, including the dominant spirit, entity, and principality that rule over this period. We live in an age of wickedness and death, but the Lord empowers His beloved to be the restraining force who pushes back the darkness. We overcome the spirit of darkness by entering into the dwelling of eternal Light, who is our Beloved. Here, we leave the spiritual battle and come into engagement with Christ to successfully collaborate with heaven and all of God's messengers to fulfill His plans for the end of the age and beyond.

We are establishing a lifestyle of drawing near to His heart in quietude and trust as He reveals His invisible attributes, eternal power, and divine nature, persuading us to fall deeper in love.

In Hosea chapter 2, God renews His covenant with Israel, promising a marriage characterized by loving kindness, tenderness, righteousness, and justice, also portraying the union that is built in engagement with Christ. This passage reads like a melody that calls for eternal betrothal and is expressed in millennial language, introducing the safety and peace that God's creation will experience in the coming age.

"Bow and sword of battle, I will shatter from the earth to make them lie down safely. I will betroth you to Me forever. Yes, I will betroth you to Me in righteousness and justice, lovingkindness and mercy. I will betroth you to Me in faithfulness, and you shall know the Lord. "It shall come to pass in that day that I will answer," says the Lord. I will answer the heavens, and they shall answer the earth. The earth shall answer with grain, with new wine, and with oil."' (Hosea 2:18-22)

The earth groans for the fulfillment of every New Covenant promise, which is our inheritance. The new grain, new wine, and oil extend beyond this age into the age to come. Grain is for the harvest of righteousness, while the wine and oil represent the Spirit of the Lord and His name. He is unveiling the essence of His name as a reward for those who overcome.

Furthermore, He reveals the remarkable truth about our engagement with Christ as we interact with Him in realms of glory for provision, restoration, and betrothal. The Lord says

He will answer the prayer from the heavens, who answers the cry of the earth, which cries for new hope and new promises.

This passage resembles the proclamation from the prophet Isaiah, which serves as a model and a guideline for Omega prayer and Omega lifestyle as we cooperate with God and His messengers to release His Words that establish the heavens, found the earth, and say to Zion, "You are My people." (Isaiah 51:16) This is engagement with Christ. This is Omega.

It is the privilege of the Omega community to contribute to the Lord's work in the restoration of the future age. Omega prayer not only builds the present day in anticipation of His appearing, but also reaches the garden for the restoration of Eden agreeing with Isaiah's prophesy, "In the time of favor I will answer You, and in the day of salvation I will help You; I will keep You and appoint You to be a covenant for the people to restore the land and to apportion its desolate inheritances." (Isaiah 49:8)

THE SCROLL OF THE FAITHFUL CHURCH

As heirs of God, we receive a taste of our inheritance now, that which is available for mortal men. The full revelation of glory is yet to come. Paul said, "For I consider that the sufferings of this present time are not worth comparing with the glory that is to be revealed to us." We have a responsibility to steward the gifts He has given, and we will receive a greater reward because of our faithfulness.

In Revelation 3, the Lord reveals the eternal scroll of the faithful church and promises divine recompense for the righteous who overcome. They are given many rewards for honoring His name and remaining faithful to His Word. The rewards that pertain to eternal purpose indicate complete appropriation and spiritual citizenship.

"Because you have a little power, and have followed My word, and have not denied My name... to the one who overcomes I will make him a pillar in the temple of My God. Never shall he go out of it, and I will write on him the name of My God, and the name of the city of My God, the New Jerusalem, which comes down from My God out of heaven, and My own new name." (Revelation 3:12)

Believing in Him, we hold fast to the name of the Lord to secure our position in the coming age. Though our salvation is secure, our position in the future age is fought for as we overcome the spirit of this current culture. Our ultimate purpose does transcend our earthly role as mortal men, though what we do on earth determines our eternal destiny. John wrote,

"These things I have written to you who believe in the name of the Son of God, that you may know that you have eternal life, and that you may continue to believe in the name of the Son of God." (1 John 5:13)

Believing in His name unlocks the pathway to eternal purpose. Holding fast to His name secures the promise. Ultimately, the promise becomes inescapable when He writes His new name upon us. As scripture, once penned, retains binding force, so it is when He writes upon us the name of God, the city of God, and His new name. Up until we receive the new name, it is possible to be erased from the Book of Life. Once His name is written upon us, it secures our place as the Holy City. Now, we move into complete oneness.

ENGRAVED BY HIS IMAGE

We are born of His image, like that of a phantom and a mere resemblance of His nature, then rebirthed into His image through salvation, ultimately becoming the complete image of God when He writes the names upon us. This is not only an identification but is a covenant of eternal union. The power in the new name is beyond comprehension for our mortal minds. It holds every concealed attribute of God, which will be revealed through our emergence into Him.

We are maturing into the full nature and power of God as we overcome the desires of the flesh and the spirit of this wicked age. For those who keep the word of His perseverance, we will receive all the attributes of the new Name, which will be written on us. Though we do not know, nor can we, fathom how great the attributes of the new Name any more than those who operated in the old covenant could understand the operation of the new covenant, which was revealed through the death and resurrection of the Lamb of God and by His blood. Nonetheless, there were forerunners who received a revelation of new covenant promises that they themselves would not walk in, though they believed. God had provided something better so that apart from us they would not be made perfect (Hebrews

11). We receive our complete inheritance together. Likewise, it requires His new name for all of us to be united, as one city, New Jerusalem, which is the dwelling of peace.

By the power and authority of the New Name, we will no longer operate as we have been, attempting to walk side by side in agreement. Instead, we will be one, whole unit. The New name of the Lord empowers this union, enabling us to dwell all as one city as the Light of the Lamb shines from our midst, and our gates will never be shut. Those who overcome have true experiential knowledge of God, as evidenced by their refusal to deny His name. They will now receive the glorious gift of His complete essence, and He will leave upon us a divine inscription of His names as a promise to dwell in peace forever, perfectly.

The principality of this age is vampirism. The enemy is using wicked humans, demonic beings, and hybrid-human alien entities to steal the essence of humanity. The essence of a person is the life, character, and attributes. The enemy is promoting self-rule and unlawful immortality. As they draw the life from the blood of God's children, they are transforming into otherworldly beings and gaining longevity of life.

According to Revelation 3, those who overcome this age and this wicked agenda will receive the Lord's new name, which includes the complete essence, life, and all character and attributes of God. Those who overcome are placed into Him when given His new name. That name and placement can never be stolen. We will know God completely and be one with His essence. This is the nature of the new name.

THE MARK OF SELF-RULE

The enemy comes as the anti-Christ, one last time, as the last great ruler of the Gentile world powers. He is given authority over every tribe, tongue, and nation, killing those who will not worship him or adopt his methods. He blasphemes the name of God, hurling insults against the sacred things of God, which are His name, His Tabernacle, and His people who dwell in heaven. The very things the anti-Christ targets through blasphemy are the very gifts God gives His overcoming bride: the name of God and the dwelling place of God.

The devil does not have a life essence. Essence is of the Spirit of life, which comes from God, and gives life to ensouled beings. The devil pulls essence out of humankind to gain his power and energy. In the original garden, Lucifer lured Eve into union with him by promising her self-rule and the knowledge of all things. As she pursued this agenda, she fueled the Luciferian energy. The anti-Christ will be the same way. He will be empowered by the idolatry and self-rule of the people and will promote it through Mystery Babylon, ultimately destroying that system to reign in full power over the people and draw them into worshipping him. His reign is short-lived.

The beast exercises authority over the people through deception, marking those whose names are not written in the book of life and have bought into the methods of the anti-Christ, which will merit a just punishment. The mark of the beast is a spiritual mark forming his image upon the people who have welcomed and worshiped the characteristics of Satan. Those who receive the mark receive undeniable identification from the anti-Christ and the nature of the beast. It is an irrefutable connection between the devil himself and those who receive the mark, claiming their eternal punishment. Ultimately, receiving the same judgment as the devil to be thrown into Gehenna (the Lake of Fire).

The numbers of the mark are discernible for those who have understanding and a reckoning with spiritual responsibility. The numbers 600, 60, and 6, being the number of man, indicate a mark for a race estranged from God, accountable to and powerless to achieve righteousness. Instead, they became a race of self-rule. They are marked with the number of self and no longer redeemable or able to surrender earthly assets for heavenly gain. It is to be marked as a mere man without the opportunity for eternal life in God or connection with God.

Ultimately, the beast is seized, and with him the false prophet who will perform the signs in his presence, by which he will deceive those who receive the mark of the beast and those who worship his image; these two will be thrown alive into Gehenna. And the rest are killed with the sword, which comes from the mouth of Christ, who sits on a white horse. And as discussed earlier regarding Ezekiel 39, all the birds will be filled with their flesh- the flesh of kings and the blood of princes.

The Lord will bring retributive justice, and the unrighteous kings will die, and their blood consumed by the birds of the sky and the beasts of the field and just as was the case with Jezebel the wicked queen whose flesh was consumed by dogs as prophesied by Elijah and her husband Ahab who was licked up by the dogs while harlots bathed in his blood. Each a severe act of God demonstrating His judgment on unrighteousness. The supper of the great God is a triumphant feat, consummating the victory over the dragon and his allies, showing God's strength and rule over all the wicked rulers and corrupt princes for all that God's people have endured for many generations.

HIS NAME IS FAITHFUL AND TRUE

Christ the Lord is faithful and true. In righteousness, He judges and makes war. The Lord in splendor will ride forth on His white horse in victory on behalf of truth and justice to judge the world with righteousness. From His mouth comes a sharp sword, so that with it He may strike down the nations.

Although He is slow to anger, God is great in power; even the clouds of the whirlwind are the dust of His feet. He will not be mocked. He reserves wrath for His enemies and wrath for the unrighteous whose heart is obstinate and shameless and unworthy to dwell with God and have stored up wrath that will count against them in the day God's judgment is revealed and His fury is poured out like fire.

Even in the age to come, the Lord gives and takes away, bringing famine to the lands of the unrighteous who refuse to worship the King and honor His feast, the feast of Tabernacles (Zechariah 14:17). His judgment is compliant with His nature and aligned with His desire, which is for His family to tabernacle with Him. The judgments of God are to bring the family of God into perfect unity.

A BRIDE ADORNED

We are motivated by the Spirit of Life to commune with God. This was the beckon in the garden. The original garden was a dwelling place for perfect love, where the first humans, created in the image of God, walked in union with God in a throne room atmosphere, with the Tree of Life in their midst. The Tree of Life is the presence of the Lord Jesus Christ, who is the Spirit of Life. In the beginning was the Word, and the Word was with God, and the Word was God. In the beginning was God, the Son, and the Spirit of Life. The Tree of Life has the power to draw humanity into union with God. The same power that is in the name of the Son. It is the power of Life in Christ. The power and nature of Christ are available to us, though we are not yet operating in the fullness as it was available in full measure in the garden, in the beginning.

Part of the splendor involving last-day ministry is the unveiling of all mysteries reserved for this age of mankind in preparation for the Lord's appearing. Paul referenced this in Ephesians 3 when he stated that to him, as the least of all saints, a wonderful grace was given to preach the unfathomable riches of Christ. Furthermore, this privilege and responsibility was to bring to light the administration of God's mystery, which for ages past "was hidden in God who created all things." Clearly, there were extraordinary revelations concerning God's plan for humanity.

Ultimate power and authority are in the Name of the Son. He is the Spirit of the Lord and is the fullness of the sevenfold Spirit of God. The Life in the Tree amid the garden is the life that is in His name. By the power of the Name, we live and dwell in

God. This is the nature of the garden at the beginning, where in union they dwelt in God's presence by the power that is in the tree of Life. This union is First Love. It is Life in union with Christ. Eden restored is our return to first love, where we will dwell in perfect union with Him. This union is a foretaste of what we will experience for eternity beyond Eden, when the new heavens and the new earth appear and we, as the Holy City, come out of heaven like a bride adorned for her husband.

THE ROYAL DAUGHTER OF EDEN

The royal daughter of Eden is the bride being adorned for true intimacy; Mystical and courageous with a mystery the current age cannot fathom, for she is energized by the wisdom of God, which is power to her soul. Her God-given independence is one of her greatest assets; yet she knows that the goal is not for isolation or singleness, but union.

She beautifies herself with the sevenfold nature of the King as one engaged to Him, eating the scroll of His word and drawing from the fruit of the future land, which keeps her strong amidst the darkest age and the church's filthiest ignorance. *This is adornment*. When he comes, she will be prepared for His appearing, adorned with joy and gladness, moving towards Him to whom she is betrothed, in a gown of fine linen woven with threads of gold, which is the oil of God.

In queenliness, she is brought to the King, who will lavish her with His kind intentions, as are the ways of a gentle King. And the royal daughter will receive her crown. She is glorious within the palace of God, as a pillar sculptured in palace style when she becomes the wife of the Lamb.

"Then He said to me, "It is done. I am the Alpha and the Omega, the beginning and the end. I will give water to the one who thirsts from the spring of the water of life, without cost. The one who overcomes will inherit these things, and I will be his God, and he will be My son. But for the cowardly, and unbelieving, and abominable, and murderers, and sexually immoral persons, and sorcerers, and idolaters, and all liars, their part *will be* in the lake that burns with fire and brimstone, which is the second death. Then one of the seven angels who had the seven bowls, full of the seven last plagues, came and spoke with me, saying, "Come here, I will show you the bride, the wife of the Lamb." (Revelation 21)

Acknowledgments

Several years ago, the Lord revealed His plan to gather the Omega team. He brought us together, humbled us, quieted our souls, put us in our positions, and taught that in quietude and trust is our strength. I want to thank the Omega Prayer family for taking your positions in God so that Paul Keith and I can take ours. Thank you for waiting on Him to hear His heart before you make your declarations—this alignment has changed the world. Thank you for holding the line, prophesying into the heavens, and for believing in His power through this generation.

A special thank you to multi-award-winning author and friend John L. Moore and Debra Moore. Thank you, Deb, for holding the line in prayer and loving well. John, for your honesty and revelatory insights that helped make Beyond Eden possible. Thank you for pushing me to grow as an author.

Sherry Furlow for standing in strength and courage all of your days. For fighting for this generation and standing with those who hurt. The Lord honors you. Thank you for your unceasing love, support, and prayers for our family.

I want to thank my dad for his inspiring courage. He overcame fear by the Spirit of Truth just days before he went to be with the Lord. Dad, I'll see you soon— at the resurrection.

Thank you, Mom, for letting me be me and encouraging me to create, write, and think. I know how you sacrificed on my behalf. You helped make me strong.

A huge thanks to my amazing kids, Elissa and Elijah, for inspiring me to love deeply. You are both so easy to love. You are the generation of the end. Take the words from God in this book and read them continually to remind you who you are. You are loved. You are free. You are emerging into your eternal purpose in Him.

A very special acknowledgment for my husband and partner in this life, Paul Keith Davis, for helping me ground each revelation deeply in the Word and listening to me process each one for hours and hours. You have encouraged me to dream and write and dream again. Thank you. You have paid a great price to carry and release this message for decades. God is pleased with how you have stood for truth. I am excited to see the Lord teach us more about His love in the coming days. I do not fly without you. I love you.

Eltis, David. Woodruff, Robert W. "The Trans-Atlantic Slave Trade Database." Slave Voyages, 14 March 2024, https://www.slavevoyages.org/blog/methodology-trans-atlantic. 3 August 2025.

Fry, Debi. "Child sexual exploitation and abuse is a multi-billion-dollar industry – and our new report shows who benefits." Childlight Global Child Safety Institute, 10 April 2025, https://www.childlight.org/newsroom/child-sexual-exploitation-and-abuse-is-a-multibillion-dollar-industry-our-new-report-shows-who-benefits. 25 June 2025.

"National Children's Alliance. (n.d.). Resources for Child Advocacy Centers." National Children's alliance, Retrieved from https://www.nationalchildrensalliance.org/. 25 June 2025.

Kreps, Daniel. "Travis Scott's Circus Maximus Concert had Roman's fearing earthquakes." Rolling Stones, 10 August 2023, https://www.rollingstone.com/music/music-news/travis-scotts-circus-maximus-concert-earthquakes-1234804479/. 3 August 2025.

Savage, Mark. "Travis Scott breaks silence on Astroworld tragedy." BBC, 16 November 2023, https://www.bbc.com/news/articles/cd1pd66y9k6o 3 August 2025

Scott, Travis. Interview by Jimmy Fallon. Tonight's Show with Jimmy Fallon. Season 11, Episode 53.